NELSON ENGLISH

Language & Writing

Don Aker

David Hodgkinson

 I(T)P Nelson

I(T)P®

International Thomson Publishing, 1999

The trademark ITP is used under licence.

www.thomson.com

ISBN 0-17-618681-6

Cataloguing in Publication Data

Aker, Don, 1955-
    Language & writing 9

ISBN 0-17-618681-6

1. English language – Grammar – Juvenile
literature. 2. English language – Composition
and exercises – Juvenile literature.
I. Hodgkinson, Dave. II. Title. III. Language
and writing nine.

PE1112.A39 1999   428.2   C99-930743-6

Publisher: Carol Stokes
Project Editor: Laurel Bishop
Series Editor: Chelsea Donaldson
Reviewer/Editor: Anthony Luengo
Art Direction: Liz Harasymczuk
Cover/Section Design: Ken Davies
Media Consultant: Nora Quinn
Composition: Carol Magee
Production Coordinator: Renate McCloy
Permissions: Vicky Gould

Reviewers
The authors and publishers gratefully
acknowledge the contributions of the following
educators:

Sandy Bender   Owen Davis
Ottawa, Ontario   London, Ontario

Mike Budd   Lilia D'Ovidio
Windsor, Ontario   Mississauga, Ontario

Anne Carrier   Irene Heffel
Toronto, Ontario   Edmonton, Alberta

Arlene Christie   Mark LaFleur
Calgary, Alberta   Ottawa, Ontario

Cathy Costello   Lisa Taylor
Aurora, Ontario   Whitby, Ontario

Printed and bound in Canada
2 3 4 5 /ML/ 03 02 01 00 99

Welcome
to *Nelson Language & Writing*

Welcome to *Nelson Language & Writing*, specially designed to boost your language skills and improve your writing. Here is what you will find inside ...

Variety! Each section focuses on one genre: narration, description, exposition, or persuasion, and is divided into three units. Every unit contains a model or models that illustrate a particular writing form and that provide a basis for the lessons that follow.

Unit 10 Comparison

What is a comparison?

A comparison is a powerful writing technique used in all subjects across the curriculum to identify similarities and differences between or among two or more people, places, actions, or things. Comparisons may be descriptive, expository, or persuasive. Their purpose may be to analyze, differentiate, define, explain, evaluate, inform, persuade—or even to entertain, as the following essay illustrates.

Learning Goals

- write a comparison
- use comparative and superlative forms of adjectives and adverbs correctly
- use colons, semicolons, and dashes correctly
- recognize and correct errors in comparison sentences
- learn to use homophones correctly

A brief introduction helps you get your bearings ...

This feature previews the language and writing skills you'll be learning.

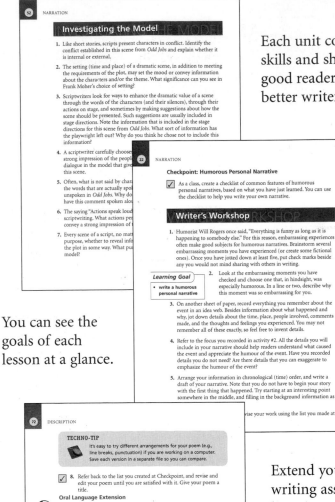

Each unit covers reading skills and shows how being a good reader can make you a better writer.

We've included lots of activities that allow you to practise new skills.

You can see the goals of each lesson at a glance.

Extend your reading and writing assignment to include listening and speaking skills.

Grammar, Mechanics, Usage & Style, and Word Study & Spelling lessons are related directly to the models and/or to the writing tasks you're working on.

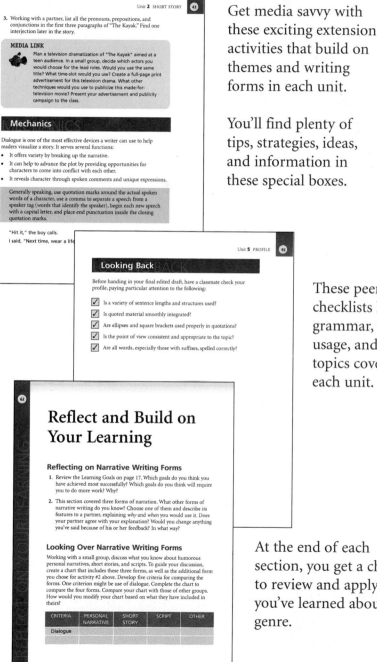

Unit **2** SHORT STORY 43

3. Working with a partner, list all the pronouns, prepositions, and conjunctions in the first three paragraphs of "The Kayak." Find one interjection later in the story.

MEDIA LINK

Plan a television dramatization of "The Kayak" aimed at a teen audience. In a small group, decide which actors you would choose for the lead roles. Would you use the same title? What time-slot would you use? Create a full-page print advertisement for this television drama. What other techniques would you use to publicize this made-for-television movie? Present your advertisement and publicity campaign to the class.

Mechanics

Dialogue is one of the most effective devices a writer can use to help readers visualize a story. It serves several functions:

- It offers variety by breaking up the narrative.
- It can help to advance the plot by providing opportunities for characters to come into conflict with each other.
- It reveals character through spoken comments and unique expressions.

Generally speaking, use quotation marks around the actual spoken words of a character, use a comma to separate a speech from a speaker tag (words that identify the speaker), begin each new speech with a capital letter, and place end punctuation inside the closing quotation marks.

"Hit it," the boy calls.
I said, "Next time, wear a life

Unit **5** PROFILE 95

Looking Back

Before handing in your final edited draft, have a classmate check your profile, paying particular attention to the following:

☑ Is a variety of sentence lengths and structures used?
☑ Is quoted material smoothly integrated?
☑ Are ellipses and square brackets used properly in quotations?
☑ Is the point of view consistent and appropriate to the topic?
☑ Are all words, especially those with suffixes, spelled correctly?

62

Reflect and Build on Your Learning

Reflecting on Narrative Writing Forms

1. Review the Learning Goals on page 17. Which goals do you think you have achieved most successfully? Which goals do you think will require you to do more work? Why?

2. This section covered three forms of narration. What other forms of narrative writing do you know? Choose one of them and describe its features to a partner, explaining *why* and *when* you would use it. Does your partner agree with your explanation? Would you change anything you've said because of his or her feedback? In what way?

Looking Over Narrative Writing Forms

Working with a small group, discuss what you know about humorous personal narratives, short stories, and scripts. To guide your discussion, create a chart that includes these three forms, as well as the additional form you chose for activity #2 above. Develop five criteria for comparing the forms. One criterion might be use of dialogue. Complete the chart to compare the four forms. Compare your chart with those of other groups. How would you modify your chart based on what they have included in theirs?

CRITERIA	PERSONAL NARRATIVE	SHORT STORY	SCRIPT	OTHER
Dialogue				

Get media savvy with these exciting extension activities that build on themes and writing forms in each unit.

You'll find plenty of tips, strategies, ideas, and information in these special boxes.

These peer-editing checklists highlight grammar, mechanics, usage, and spelling topics covered in each unit.

At the end of each section, you get a chance to review and apply what you've learned about the genre.

Contents

Description **64**

Exposition   112

Persuasion   156

The Writing Process: An Illustration

One way to understand the writing process is to watch someone working through it. Meet Gina, a high school student, who was recently given the following assignment:

> Write an essay persuading someone to believe or to do something that is important to you.

Prewriting

When **choosing a topic**, ask yourself the following questions:

- Am I interested in this topic?
- Is my topic specific enough to cover in a single piece of writing?
- Do I know enough about this topic to write about it?
- Does this topic meet the assignment requirements?

Like most of her classmates, Gina started with no idea what to write about. She could think of lots of issues—smoking, pollution, unfair treatment of animals—but none that hadn't been repeated many times. She glanced over at her friend Nick and was surprised to see him scribbling furiously.

"I want to persuade the principal to allow us to use our skateboards in the parking lot after school hours," he explained when Gina inquired what he was writing. Gina's eyes widened. All of a sudden, now that she was thinking closer to home, Gina had lots of ideas. In particular, she remembered a discussion in French class last week about their planned trip to Montreal in the spring. Someone suggested they go canoeing on a lake in the Laurentians, as well as hiking in the area, but their teacher said the school board would not give them permission for canoeing. Gina began jotting down ideas that might convince the school board to change its mind.

School board's arguments	My counter-arguments

School board's arguments
- too dangerous; students could be hurt

- too expensive

My counter-arguments
- students can be hurt in school sports, too (need to find out details about safety of canoeing—equipment?)
- students can buy extra accident insurance
- will have parent/teacher chaperones
- students can get physical examinations proving they are healthy enough

- class has raised enough money to cover cost of this activity and others

Reasons I (we) want to go canoeing and hiking
- sounds like lots of fun
- canoeing and hiking are becoming more and more popular
- canoeing and hiking will show us the geography of the Laurentian area
- will introduce students to new outdoor activities (encourage them to be physically active)
- the trip should include activities that appeal to different interests
- it will make the trip memorable

Gina checked off the arguments she thought were most important and put numbers beside them indicating a possible order. Then she headed for the library to find information about the safety of canoeing.

When **organizing ideas**, ask yourself the following questions:
- Does the type of writing suggest a possible order?
- What order will make my ideas appealing to my audience?
- What key words will help me order my ideas?

Drafting

When **drafting**, ask yourself the following questions:
- How will I get and keep my audience's attention?
- What transition words will make my writing easy to follow?
- Are all my details relevant to my purpose and my audience?
- How can I end my piece so my purpose is clear?

The following day, Gina met with a group of her classmates to share their topics and the arguments they had decided to use. Sunil advised her not to include the idea about accident insurance because it suggested that an accident would likely happen, and Nick told her that Mr. Gerrard, his soccer coach and an avid canoeist, might be willing to help Gina in her request to the school board.

After the students had shared their ideas, the teacher gave them the remainder of the period to work on their first drafts. Gina wondered how to begin. She tried out several openings until she found one she thought worked, then continued writing. When the bell rang twenty minutes later, she stopped writing in the middle of a sentence, a trick that made it easier to begin writing again when she returned to it.

If you're finding it hard to get the words down, try
- explaining what you're trying to say to a friend
- refocusing on your purpose and your audience
- writing nonstop about anything for ten minutes
- reading or recopying what you've already written

Revising

When **revising**, ask yourself the following questions:
- Are my purpose and audience clear?
- What do I like best about my writing?
- Are there parts that I don't like? Why not?
- Does every part of the writing relate to my purpose?
- Is there anything missing?

Gina finished the first draft of her essay on the computer later that evening. She resisted the temptation to revise it right away, though, because she knew that she needed a little distance from it before she could be objective. She put it into her writing folder and planned to return to it in a couple of days.

Later that week, Gina took out the hard copy of her essay and sat down with a pencil in hand. She liked to work directly on the paper and make the changes on the computer later so that, if she deleted something that she later decided to use, it would still be on disk.

As she began to read, Gina frowned. Her opening was a conversation between her and Sunil in which they complained about adults not remembering what it was like to be a teenager. She had been pleased with it at the time, but now it sounded insulting. She circled the opening and put a question mark by it, then read through the rest of her draft, concentrating on its focus, content, and organization.

Writing is **focused** if
- it is structured to emphasize the main point
- it achieves the purpose you set out to achieve
- it is directed at the audience for whom you set out to write

When checking the **content** of your writing, make sure
- everything you say helps you to achieve your purpose
- you've included enough information for your audience
- you haven't included any unnecessary information

When revising the **order** of your writing, decide if
- the information is arranged to suit your purpose and audience
- any paragraphs or sentences should be added, deleted, or rearranged to make your points more effectively

When Gina tried to imagine the school board members' reactions to her ideas, she began to notice other areas where her remarks sounded insulting, as well as a few places where she needed to include more information. She also realized that her argument about wanting to make the trip memorable wasn't convincing because there were many other activities they could try besides canoeing and hiking. She got her disk and went to the computer.

The next day in class, the other members of Gina's writers' group reminded her that her strongest argument should appear last because that was the one her audience would remember best. They all felt her argument about encouraging physically active lifestyles was her strongest, and Gina decided she would need to rethink the order of her ideas.

Editing and Proofreading

When **editing and proofreading**, ask yourself the following questions:
- Have I used as few words as possible to achieve my purpose?
- Are my words well chosen, given my audience and purpose?
- Are my sentences clear?
- What particular grammar, mechanics, usage, and spelling errors should I check for?

Now that Gina had made all the changes to the content of her piece she felt were necessary, she took out the list of writing errors her class had been focusing on that term, paying close attention to the ones she found especially difficult. She found only a few errors, but still planned to have Sunil proofread it for her the next day in class—Gina was sure there were some errors she just couldn't see herself.

When she had finished, Gina printed off a polished version of her essay and read it again. This time, though, she wasn't looking for problems. This time, she was just enjoying having written. Even if her arguments didn't convince the school board, she was confident she had written her best essay ever.

Healthy Bodies, Healthy Minds

We look at the sun shining on the lake, mesmerized by the beauty of our surroundings, and proud of the fact that we have worked as a team to canoe across the lake. "Isn't this terrific?" says my friend Sunil. Well, I think, as I sit staring across the classroom at her now, it would be—that is, if you and the other members of the school board would give our class permission to go canoeing during our trip to Montreal this spring.

Yes, canoeing carries some risks, but so does every high school team sport. Bruises, sprained ankles, broken arms—all these injuries happen daily in school gyms and on playing fields across Canada, yet all schools agree that sports are an important part of a student's education. The risks involved in canoeing can be minimized by the use of special safety equipment such as life-jackets. Most canoeing companies require that participants be able to swim; students who wish to take part would be asked to provide the school board with proof of their swimming ability before we left.

In researching this sport, I discovered that most canoeing accidents result from horseplay and a lack of familiarity with the hazards involved. We can take many steps to ensure that such horseplay does not occur. For example, all participants can sign behaviour contracts stating that they understand the risks involved and will conduct themselves accordingly. Also, when arranging the event, we can make sure that parent volunteers who are familiar with canoeing be present and take part. Most important, though, we can learn more about canoeing long before the trip even takes place. Keith Gerrard, our soccer coach, has canoed many times and has agreed to conduct after-school workshops for interested students.

Education is most meaningful when it is student centred, appealing to the particular interests, abilities, and talents of individual students. During the day the students who have chosen the outdoor activities are away, the remainder of the class could tour the Musée des beaux-arts de Montréal as well as other cultural centres. This arrangement would allow people to take part in experiences that appeal specifically to them, after which we can all share our different experiences with each other.

One of the most important goals of education is to develop a well-rounded individual, one who is physically active as well as literate. Allowing students to take part in canoeing and hiking would encourage students to participate in a variety of recreational activities, not just now but in the years ahead. Exposing students to these activities is an excellent way to encourage students to adopt a physically active lifestyle and, in the process, to become the well-rounded individuals that society needs.

As elected members of the school board, you are obviously committed to providing your students with educational experiences that will benefit them now and in the future. By granting permission for my class to go on this outing, you not only will be ensuring that our trip to Montreal is memorable, you will be demonstrating your faith in us as sound decision-makers. We will not disappoint you.

Narration

Narration is storytelling. We use narration not only in novels and short stories, but every time we share an experience with others. In fact, stories—both fictional and nonfictional—are how we make sense of our world, in everything from myths to news reports, from historical accounts to friendly chatter in the cafeteria.

This section contains three forms of narrative writing, one autobiographical and two fictional: a humorous personal narrative, a short story, and a script excerpt. Each is written about a different subject and from a different perspective, but they all tell a story in a way that is interesting, entertaining, and leaves the reader asking "What happened next?"

Features of Narration

- A narrative is a story developed from an event or series of events.
- Narratives usually involve a character in conflict.
- Details of character, setting, conflict, and plot are usually chosen and ordered in such a way as to develop a main theme, or idea.
- The beginning of the story usually establishes the characters, setting, and mood.
- The middle of the narrative describes events in which the character deals with the main conflict and other minor conflicts.
- The end of the story tells how the conflict is resolved.

Learning Goals

- use print and electronic sources to gather information and explore ideas for your written work

- identify and use literary forms appropriately in writing a humorous personal narrative, a short story, and a scene for a script

- use organizational techniques to present ideas and supporting details

- revise your written work independently and collaboratively

- edit and proofread to produce final drafts using correct grammar, spelling, and punctuation

- use knowledge of vocabulary and language conventions; for example, use nouns, verbs, adverbs, and adjectives correctly

- develop listening, speaking, and media literacy skills

- read a variety of fiction, such as humorous personal narrative, short story, and script

- identify and understand the elements and style of a variety of fiction

Unit 1 Humorous Personal Narrative

What is a humorous personal narrative?

A personal narrative is a brief account of an event the writer has experienced. In a humorous personal narrative, the writer's purpose is to amuse the reader by emphasizing the comic nature of the event. In the following narrative, noted Canadian author Margaret Atwood entertains readers with her "first moment of truly public embarrassment."

Learning Goals

- write a humorous personal narrative
- use parts of speech correctly: nouns, verbs, adverbs, and adjectives
- use commas correctly
- use consistent and appropriate verb tense
- identify words borrowed from other languages

A Flying Start

BY MARGARET ATWOOD

IN ADULT LIFE, MY MOST EMBARRASSING MOMENTS HAVE come during other people's introductions to my readings. What do you do when the man introducing you proposes to read the audience the entire last chapter of your novel, gets your name wrong, or characterizes you as some kind of machine-gun-wielding radical terrorist?

But my first moment of truly public embarrassment occurred when I was 14. It was the early days of CBC Television, and things were kind of improvised. Many shows were live. There was usually just one camera; there was little editing. Much joy was contributed to the world, in those days, by the howlers, faux pas, bloopers, and pratfalls that were sent out, uncensored, over the airwaves.

The woman who lived next door, and for whom I babysat, had somehow become the producer of a show called *Pet Corner,* a title that is self-explanatory. At that time, in lieu of cats, I had a beautiful, green, intelligent praying mantis called Lenore (after the Poe poem, not after my future sister-in-law), which lived in a large jar, ate insects, and drank sugar water out of a spoon. (For those who may accuse me of cruelty to insects, let me point out that this was a) an old praying mantis, which had b) already laid its egg-mass, and which c) lived a good deal longer in my jar than it would have outside, as it was d) cold out there.) My neighbour thought this would be a good thing to have on *Pet Corner* so I went, praying mantis, spoon, and all, and presumably electrified the audience with an account of what female praying mantises would eat if they could get any, namely male praying mantises.

Lenore was such a hit that *Pet Corner* decided to have me back. This time I was to be merely an adjunct. A woman was coming onto the show with a tame flying squirrel; I was to be the person the flying squirrel flew to, a sort of human tree.

All went as scheduled up to the time of the flight. Flying squirrels were explained, this one was produced (close shot), then raised on high, aimed, and fired. But flying squirrels are nocturnal, and it was annoyed by the bright television lights. When it landed on me, it immediately went down my front.

At my school we wore uniforms: black stockings, bloomers, white blouses, and a short tunic with a belt and a large square neckline. It was this neckline that the squirrel utilized; it then began scrabbling around beneath and could be seen as a travelling bulge moving around my waistline, above the belt (close shot). But it was looking for something even more secluded. I thought of the bloomers, and swiftly reached down the front of my own neckline. Then I thought better of it, and began to lift the skirt. Then I thought better of that as well. Paralysis. Nervous giggling. At last the owner of the flying squirrel fished the thing out via the back of my jumper.

Luckily the show went on during school hours, so none of my classmates saw it. Not much that has gone on at public readings since then has been able to compete in embarrassment value; not even the times I fell off the podium, had a nosebleed, or had to be whacked on the back by James Reaney because I was choking to death. Maybe it's for that reason that I always have trouble spelling "embarrassment." I keep thinking it should have three e's. ■

Investigating the Model

1. The main purpose of most humorous personal narratives is simply to entertain the reader. Did you find the model narrative entertaining? Tell why or why not.

2. The personal narrative usually begins by quickly establishing the writer as a credible narrator and arousing interest by identifying the nature of the event he or she will recount. Does Atwood's introduction succeed in doing both? Explain.

3. Humorous personal narratives often centre around typical characters: the helpless victim of circumstances, the neurotic, and the naive or innocent individual. Which of these character types does Atwood adopt in presenting her narrative? How do you know?

4. Like most stories, the details of a personal narrative are often arranged in chronological order. Does Atwood follow this organizational pattern? Give examples to support your response.

5. Unlike longer narratives, the humorous personal narrative focuses on a single event. Why do you think Atwood included information about her first appearance on *Pet Corner* when, in fact, her most embarrassing moment occurred during her second appearance?

6. The humorous personal narrative is usually told from a first-person point of view. Evaluate the effectiveness of this point of view in Atwood's narrative. How might the impact of the piece have been different if she had told the story in the third person?

7. One way authors of narratives "show" rather than "tell" their experiences is to include the actual words spoken by the people involved. Atwood uses no dialogue in her narrative. What spoken comments might she have included in her account of the squirrel incident? Why do you suppose she chose not to include them?

8. Two ways to create humour in your narrative are the use of understatement (describing events in a restrained, low-key way), and exaggeration (using extreme or overblown description). Which of these devices does Atwood use in her narrative?

9. Humorous personal narratives often end abruptly, forcing the reader to imagine the effect of the incident on the narrator. Is this true of the model? Suggest a different place where the narrative could have ended. Which version do you prefer? Why?

Checkpoint: Humorous Personal Narrative

✓ As a class, create a checklist of common features of humorous personal narratives, based on what you have just learned. You can use the checklist to help you write your own narrative.

Writer's Workshop

1. Humorist Will Rogers once said, "Everything is funny as long as it is happening to somebody else." For this reason, embarrassing experiences often make good subjects for humorous narratives. Brainstorm several embarrassing moments you have experienced (or create some fictional ones). Once you have jotted down at least five, put check marks beside any you would not mind sharing with others in writing.

Learning Goal

- **write a humorous personal narrative**

2. Look at the embarrassing moments you have checked and choose one that, in hindsight, was especially humorous. In a line or two, describe why this moment was so embarrassing for you.

3. On another sheet of paper, record everything you remember about the event in an idea web. Besides information about what happened and why, jot down details about the time, place, people involved, comments made, and the thoughts and feelings you experienced. You may not remember all of these exactly, so feel free to invent details.

4. Refer to the focus you recorded in activity #2. All the details you will include in your narrative should help readers understand what caused the event and appreciate the humour of the event. Have you recorded details you do not need? Are there details that you can exaggerate to emphasize the humour of the event?

5. Arrange your information in chronological (time) order, and write a draft of your narrative. Note that you do not have to begin your story with the first thing that happened. Try starting at an interesting point somewhere in the middle, and filling in the background information as you go.

✓ 6. Give your story a title. Revise your work using the list you made at Checkpoint.

Oral Language Extension

Standup comics recognize the importance of facial expressions (including deadpan), gestures, and intonation in delivering their monologues, and cable networks offer numerous opportunities to view standup comics practising their craft. If possible, tape a standup routine and, working with a partner, cue examples of facial expressions, gestures, and tone of voice that help engage the audience and share these with the class. Then, reduce your humorous personal narrative to its essential elements and present it to the class or a small group as a short standup monologue using these same techniques.

WRITING TIP

Here are two descriptions of the same incident, one using understatement, and the other using exaggeration. Choose one or the other of these techniques to use in your own writing.

Understated: The squirrel described a delicate arc in the air and landed lightly inside my tunic. It then proceeded, to the amusement of those present, to burrow down in an effort to avoid the lights. A light tickling sensation around my midriff kept me apprised of its whereabouts until the owner managed to remove it by reaching in the back.

Exaggerated: The squirrel panicked and leaped, jaws gaping, toward me. Digging its vicious claws into my flesh, it made a perfect landing— smack—right inside my tunic. Then, half crazed from excitement, it began tearing around inside, looking desperately for an exit. I could feel it scrabbling around, looking no doubt for a spot to begin tearing its way out with teeth and claws. Who knows what might have happened if the owner had not managed just then to reach in the back of my tunic and grab the beast!

Grammar

There are eight main word classes, or **parts of speech**. The most important of these are nouns, verbs, adjectives, and adverbs.

A **noun** is a word that names a person, place, thing, quality, or idea.

① Find the nouns in the model. Classify them under the following headings: PEOPLE, PLACES, THINGS, and QUALITIES AND IDEAS. Which column has the fewest entries? Which has the most?

Note: For more on nouns, see Unit 6.

A **verb** is a word that shows an action (**action verb**) or a state of being (**linking verb**). Sometimes a verb may be made up of more than one word: a main verb and one or more **helping** (or **auxiliary**) **verbs**.

Lenore **was** a beautiful, green, praying mantis who *ate* insects.

    state of being   *action*

My most embarrassing moments *have*   **come** during other people's introductions to my readings.

                            helping verb   **main verb**

② Find at least three other sentences in the model that contain action verbs, three that contain linking verbs, and three that contain helping verbs.

Note: For more on verbs, see Units 8 and 9.

An **adjective** describes or tells about a noun or pronoun. An **adverb** is a modifier that describes a verb, an adjective, or another adverb. When describing verbs, adverbs tell how, when, or where.

Adjectives and adverbs are called modifiers.

Adjectives: *Flying* squirrels are *nocturnal*.

Adverbs: I thought of the bloomers and *very swiftly* reached down the front of my own neckline.

In adult life, my *most* embarrassing moments have come during other people's introductions to my readings.

3. Copy three sentences from the model that contain modifiers. Circle the modifiers and draw arrows connecting the circled words to the words they modify. Identify whether the modifiers are adjectives or adverbs.

Many words can act as different parts of speech depending on the way they are used in a sentence.

> I was to be the person the flying squirrel flew to, a sort of *human* tree. (*human* is an adjective)
>
> A *human* cannot compete with a flying squirrel for an audience's attention. (*human* is a noun)

> ### Learning Goal
>
> - **use parts of speech correctly: nouns, verbs, adverbs, and adjectives**

Note: For more on modifiers, see Units 3 and 10.

4. Identify the part of speech of each of the boldface words. Then write another sentence using the same word as a different part of speech. Identify the new part of speech.
  a) What do you do when the man introducing you gets your name **wrong**?
  b) One man read the audience the entire last chapter of my **novel**.
  c) My first moment of truly **public** embarrassment occurred when I was 14.
  d) It was the early days of CBC Television, and things were kind of **improvised**.
  e) There was usually just one camera; there was little **editing**.
  f) It was annoyed by the bright **television** lights.
  g) Many shows were **live**.

Note: For more on parts of speech, see Unit 2.

MEDIA LINK

Stock characters (for example, the nosy neighbour, the "jock," the accident-prone individual) convey a lot of information quickly and are used repeatedly in many half-hour sitcoms. Identify the stock characters in one episode of a sitcom and analyze the body language, clothing, facial expressions, speech patterns, and actions used to make the stereotype immediately recognizable by the viewer.

Mechanics

Writers use commas more than any other form of punctuation. Here are some of the most important uses for a comma:

Use	Example
Between items in a series.	At my school we wore uniforms: black stockings, bloomers, white blouses, and a short tunic with a belt and a large square neckline.
To replace the word *and* between two or more adjectives.	I had a beautiful, green, intelligent praying mantis called Lenore.
After an introductory group of several words.	For those who may accuse me of cruelty to insects, let me point out that this was an old praying mantis.
To set off words that interrupt a flow of thought.	The woman who lived next door, and for whom I babysat, had somehow become the producer of a show called *Pet Corner*.
To separate two complete sentences joined by *and*, *but*, *or*, *nor*, *so*, or *yet*.	It was the early days of CBC Television, and things were kind of improvised.
To separate words or expressions that refer to the same person or thing.	A woman was coming onto the show with an unusual pet, a tame flying squirrel.
To separate a subordinate clause from the main clause that follows it.	When it landed on me, it immediately went down my front.

Note: For more on comma use, see Unit 8.

Learning Goal

- **use commas correctly**

1. Copy the following sentences, inserting commas where necessary. For each comma you include, explain the rule that makes it necessary.
   a) My next-door neighbour the producer of *Pet Corner* was impressed by Lenore.

b) Other pets on the show included a talking parrot a dancing dog and a snake.

c) Near the end of the show I pretended to be a tree for the squirrel to fly to.

d) Because the squirrel was a nocturnal animal the lights bothered it.

e) I was embarrassed as I tried to catch the frightened wriggling elusive animal.

f) The audience on the other hand found the performance very entertaining.

g) The episode with the flying squirrel happened many years ago but I still remember it clearly.

2. Working with a partner, write at least two other rules for using commas that have not been discussed and make up sentences illustrating each rule. Share your information with other groups and compare your findings.

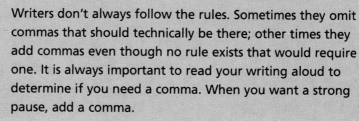

WRITING TIP

Writers don't always follow the rules. Sometimes they omit commas that should technically be there; other times they add commas even though no rule exists that would require one. It is always important to read your writing aloud to determine if you need a comma. When you want a strong pause, add a comma.

Sometimes people make the mistake of using too many commas. Do NOT use commas for the following purposes :

- to separate a verb from its subject or object
- before or after a list
- to separate a string of adjectives (except to replace the word "and")
- to separate an adjective from the noun it modifies

3. Rewrite the following passage, eliminating unnecessary commas. Refer to the points listed above.

Most Canadians recognize, Margaret Atwood, as one of our country's finest novelists, but she is also an acclaimed, short-story writer, essayist, and poet. Born in Ottawa, she began publishing her poems when she was 19. Her first book, of poetry, *Double Persephone*, was published in 1961, and she won, the Governor General's Award in 1966 for another volume, of poetry, (*The Circle Game*). She is the author, of several critically acclaimed novels. One of her best-known novels, *The Handmaid's Tale*, earned her a second, Governor General's Award in 1986. Both *The Handmaid's Tale*, and an earlier novel, *Surfacing*, have been made into films.

4. Read through your personal narrative to make sure you have used commas correctly.

Usage & Style

The **tense** of a verb refers to the time when an action is performed. Read the following passage and note how the boldface verbs in the first sentence differ from those in the second sentence.

> What do you **do** when the man introducing you **proposes** to read the audience the entire last chapter of your novel, **gets** your name wrong, or **characterizes** you as some kind of machine-gun-wielding radical terrorist?

> But my first moment of truly public embarrassment **occurred** when I **was** 14.

<table>
<tr><td>

Learning Goal

• **use consistent and appropriate verb tense**

</td></tr>
</table>

"Do," "proposes," "gets," and "characterizes" refer to a time in the present, so they are present-tense verbs. "Occurred" and "was" refer to a time in the past, so they are past-tense verbs.

Writers often use present tense to generate excitement and tension because present tense makes readers feel they are right there watching the event happen.

> Slowly, dramatically, she points the squirrel in my direction, and off he goes …

Although some writers intentionally mix both past and present verb tenses to create a particular effect, make sure you do not use two verb tenses by mistake. Choose a tense that is appropriate for your purpose and use it consistently throughout your piece of writing.

1. There is a sentence in "A Flying Start" that contains both present-tense and past-tense verbs. Find it and identify the tense of each verb. With a partner, discuss whether the author is justified in switching tenses in this case.

2. The following passage is supposed to be written in past tense, but it contains some present-tense verbs. Rewrite the passage using the correct tense throughout.

   Last year, public-access cable television has provided audiences with countless unplanned—yet highly entertaining—viewing experiences. On one show about unusual hobbies, a woman brings in three live bats to illustrate her involvement in ethology, the biological study of animal behaviour. She wanted to dispel several myths about bats, particularly the one that bats entangle themselves in women's long hair, and she removed one of the bats from its carrier and places it on her head. Just at that moment, her folding chair collapsed and the bat flies off her head and landed on the long, bushy beard of the show's host. The show ended abruptly as the host leaped up and, flailing his arms in terror, knocks the television camera to the floor.

3. Read your own humorous personal narrative and check to see that you have chosen an appropriate tense and used it consistently throughout. If you changed the tense, did you do it for a good reason?

Word Study & Spelling

Words in the English language come into being in a variety of ways. Here are a few of them:

- Existing words are borrowed from other languages such as French.

  faux pas   **lieu**

- New words are formed by arranging old words in new combinations.

  television (from the ancient Greek *tele,* meaning "far off," and the Latin word *videre,* meaning "see")

- Two existing words are combined to form a third word.

   nosebleed   **neckline**

- Words are formed by imitating sounds.

   slap   **ping**

- Acronyms, which are formed from the first letters of a group of words, become words in their own right.

   radar (*r*adio *d*etecting *a*nd *r*anging)
   modem (*mo*dulator-*dem*odulator)

- Some words are named after people or places.

   sandwich (named after the Earl of Sandwich)
   suede (from Sweden, where it originated)

- Some words are entirely invented. Many slang words come into being this way. So did **quark**, the name for the particle that scientists believe makes up protons and neutrons. It was borrowed from Irish writer James Joyce, who used it in his novel *Finnegan's Wake.*

TECHNO-TIP

You can find lots of sites devoted to word origins on the Internet if you search the key word "etymology." However, always double-check information you find on Web sites in a dictionary or other reference books.

1. a) Working with a partner, find at least three other French words or expressions in the dictionary that are commonly used in English.

   b) Can you think of words or expressions we commonly use that come directly from other languages? Consider Aboriginal, Italian, German, and others. Make a list and share it with others in the class. Combine your lists to create a class database of borrowed words.

2. In her narrative "A Flying Start," Margaret Atwood uses words that were created using all the methods described above. Read the narrative again and identify at least one example of each method.

Knowing how a word was formed can be a big help when you are trying to figure out how to spell an unfamiliar word. For example, if you know the word *physical* and the suffix *-ology,* you will know how to spell *physiology.*

3. a) List several recent technological inventions and, using a dictionary, determine the origins of their names. Mix and match the different parts of the words to create new words. Then, write a definition based on the meanings of the word parts. Make your new words humorous if you wish.

　　b) Share your new words and their definitions out loud with a group of other students. Challenge them to spell the word correctly, using their knowledge of other words with the same word origins. Listen to other people's words and do the same.

WORD ORIGINS

The word *embarrass* originally meant "to impede." It comes from the Italian word *imbarrazzare*, which literally means "to confine within bars." Today we use this word to mean "to make someone self-conscious." What connection can you see between these uses of the word?

Looking Back

Before handing in your final edited draft, have a classmate check your personal narrative, paying particular attention to the following:

 Are commas used correctly?

 Are verbs written in a correct and consistent tense?

✓ Are all words spelled correctly?

Unit **2** Short Story

What is a short story?

A short story is a work of prose fiction that presents a main character involved in a single episode that begins, develops, and ends in a limited space. In sharing the main character's experience, the short story writer shows the reader an understanding about life and living. In the following story by Debbie Spring, a 16-year-old girl confronts both an outer and inner storm as she kayaks on Georgian Bay.

Learning Goals

- **write a short story**
- **use parts of speech correctly: pronouns, prepositions, conjunctions, and interjections**
- **punctuate and capitalize dialogue correctly**
- **identify elements of foreshadowing in short stories**
- **identify how words change over time**

The Kayak

BY DEBBIE SPRING

THE CHOPPY WAVES RISE AND FALL. I RIDE THE WAVE. MY kayak bobs like a cork in the swirling waters of Georgian Bay. I love it. I feel wild and free. The wind blows my hair into my eyes. I concentrate on my balance. *It's more difficult now.* I stop stroking with my double-bladed paddle and push my bangs from my face.

This is my special place. Out here, I feel safe and secure. My parents watch from the shore. I have on my life jacket and emergency whistle. I am one with the kayak. The blue boat is an extension of my legs. I can do anything: I can go anywhere. Totally independent. Totally in control of my life. It's so different back on shore.

I approach Cousin Island, where I have to steer around the submerged rocks. In the shallows, a school of large-mouth bass darts between the weeds. A wave pushes me toward the rocks. I push off with my paddle and I head out toward the middle of Kilcoursie Bay. Powerful swirls of wind and current toss me about.

The clouds move in, warning signs. I turn the kayak and head back to shore. The waves peak wildly as the storm picks up. My arms ache.

I don't want to go back to the shore. Nobody lets me grow up. My parents treat me like a baby. I'm 16, too old to be pampered. I'm already a woman.

Just off my bow, a loon preens its black mottled feathers. It sounds its piercing cry and disappears under the water. I hold my breath, waiting for it to resurface. Time slows. Finally, it reappears in the distance. I exhale.

I notice a windsurfer with a flashy neon green and purple sail, gaining on me. My stomach does flip-flops as he races, dangerously close. "Look out," I yell. I quickly steer out of the way. He just misses me. *Stupid kid, he's not even wearing a life jacket.* I shake my head. The boy is out of control. He's heading straight for the rocks at Cousin Island. "Drop the sail!" I call.

He does and not a second too soon. He just misses a jagged rock. I slice through the waves and grab onto his white surfboard.

"Can you get back to shore?" I ask.

"The windsurfer belongs to my buddy. It's my first time. I don't know how." His voice trembles. Is it from the cold?

The windsurfer looks around 18. I take a quick glance at his tanned muscles and sandy, blond hair. He seems vulnerable and afraid. His blue eyes narrow. "Now what?" he asks.

I reach into the cockpit and take out a rope. "Hold on." I toss the rope. He misses. I throw it again and he catches it. "Paddle to my stern with your hands." His board moves directly behind me. "Tie the other end through that yellow loop." I point.

He fumbles for what seems like several painful minutes. "Got it."

I stroke hard, straining to move us.

"Hit it," the boy calls.

"What?"

"That's what you shout, in water skiing, when you're ready to take off."

I smile. Slowly, we make our way. My paddle dips into the water, first to the right, then to the left. Beads of sweat form on my forehead. Suddenly, I surge ahead. I turn around. "You let go." I circle and give him back the rope. "Wrap it around your wrist."

"Sorry."

"It's okay. What's your name?"

"Jamie." His teeth chatter. The water churns around his board. He is soaked. I don't like the blue colour of his lips.

"I'm Teresa. Don't worry, Jamie. It will be slow because we're going against the current. I promise to get you back in one piece." It takes too much energy to talk. Instead, I get him chatting. "Tell me about yourself."

"I thought I was good at all water sports, but windsurfing sure isn't one of them," he laughs.

I don't mean to answer. It just comes out. "Maybe with practice."

"Dumb to go out so far. I don't know what I'm doing." He changes the rope to the other hand, flexing the stiff one.

The wind changes. A big wave hits Jamie sideways, knocking him into the dark, chilly water. He shoots to the top for air and tangles in my slack rescue rope.

He is trapped underneath the sail.

"Jamie!" I scream. The wind swallows my voice. Quickly, I position my boat perpendicular to his board, like a T. I drop my paddle, grabbing the tip of his sail at the mast. I tug. Nothing. The water on top of the sail makes it heavy. I drop it. I try again. One, two, three, heave. I grunt as I break the air pocket and lift the sail a couple of inches. It's enough to let Jamie wriggle out. He explodes to the surface, gulping in air. He pulls himself safely onto the surfboard. I reach over to help untangle the rope from around his foot. I can see an ugly rope burn.

My kayak starts to tip. I throw my weight to the opposite side to keep from flipping. My heart beats fast. "Keep hold of the rope."

"Got it."

"Where's my paddle?" My throat tightens. I search the water. "There it is," I sigh with relief. It's floating a few feet away. My hands pull through the water, acting like paddles. I reach out and grab the shaft of my paddle.

"Hang on, Jamie." The waves swell. The current changes and we ride the waves like a bucking bronco.

I have to keep away from shore or the waves will crash us against the granite, splitting us in half. Just as we clear the rocks, a crosscurrent hits me. My kayak flips. I'm sitting upside down in the water. *Don't panic. Do the roll.* I get my paddle in the ready position. Then I swing the blade away from the boat's side. I arch my back around and through, keeping my head low. I sweep my blade through the water, pulling hard. I right the kayak and gasp for breath.

"You gave me a heart attack." Jamie looks white.

"Caught me by surprise." We drift, while I catch my breath. The clouds turn black. The water becomes dead calm.

"For now, it will be easy going. It's going to storm any minute." I paddle fast and hard. The rain comes down in buckets.

"I'm already wet, so it doesn't matter," Jamie jokes.

I like his sense of humour, but I'm not used to talking to a guy. I've never had a boyfriend. Who would be interested in me?

"You don't know what it's like being so helpless," Jamie says.

I bite my lip. The kayak drifts. I see my parents waving from shore.

My father runs into the water to help. Everything happens real fast. He takes control. Before I know it, Jamie and I are safely back. My mother runs over with towels. Jamie wraps the towel around himself and pulls the windsurfer onto the sand. I stay in my kayak. Half the kayak is on land. The rest is in the water. I feel trapped, like a beached whale.

A turkey vulture circles above me, decides I'm not dead and flies away. I feel dead inside.

Jamie comes back and stands over me. "Do you need help?" he asks.

I shake my head, no. *Go away!* I scream in my head. *Go away, everybody*!

"Thanks for saving my skin," Jamie says.

"Next time, wear a life jacket."

Jamie doesn't flinch. "You're right. That was dumb." It is pouring even harder. Jamie hugs the wet towel around him. "Aren't you getting out?" he asks.

"Yes." Tears sting my eyes, mixed with the rain. My mother pushes a wheelchair over. My father lifts me. A blanket is wrapped around my shivering shoulders. I motion for my parents to leave me alone. Surprised, they move away, but stay close by. Jamie stares.

"Say something." My voice quivers. A fat bullfrog croaks and jumps into the water. I want to jump in after him and swim away somewhere safe. I say nothing more.

"Teresa," he clears his throat. "I didn't know."

I watch his discomfort. I've seen it all before. Awkwardness. Forced conversation. A feeble excuse and a fast getaway. My closer friends tried a little harder. They lasted two or three visits. Then, they stopped coming around.

The silence drags on. A mosquito buzzes around my head. So annoying. Why can't they both leave? It lands on my arm and I smack it.

"Do you like roasting marshmallows?" asks Jamie.

"Huh?"

"I like mine burnt to a crisp."

I hate small talk. My hands turn white as I clutch the armrests of my wheelchair. "What you really want to know is how long I've been crippled."

Jamie winces. He doesn't say anything. I wish he would leave. The air feels heavy and suffocating. I decide to make it easy for him. I'll go first. I push on the wheels with my hands. The sand is wet. The wheels bury, instead of thrusting the wheelchair forward. I stop pushing. Another helpless moment. My parents are watching, waiting for my signal to look after me.

Jamie puts his hand on my shoulder. "Would you like to join me and my friends at a campfire tonight?"

"I don't need pity," I retort.

Jamie smiles. "Actually, I need a date. Everybody is a couple, except me. Where's your campsite?"

"Granite Saddle number 1026." *Why do I tell him? What's the matter with me?* I stare at my wheelchair and then at my kayak. My eyes water. Through tears, I see two images of me: the helpless child on land and the independent woman on water. I blink and the land and water merge. I become one.

I smile back at him.

Jamie pushes me past my parents. They stare at me, in confusion.

"It's okay. I'll take Teresa to your campsite." My parents walk behind at a safe distance, moving slowly, despite the rain. We stop at my tent. I smell the fragrance of wet pine needles.

"I'll pick you up at nine." An ember flickers in the wet fireplace, catching our eyes. Sparks rise up into the sky. Jamie takes my hand.

"One other thing."

"Yes?" I choke out.

"Bring the marshmallows." ■

Investigating the Model

1. The lead of a short story should catch the reader's attention, identify the main character, introduce the conflict (the problem the main character faces), define the setting, and establish the point of view (who is telling the story). Does the lead of "The Kayak" accomplish all these things? Explain.

2. The plot of most stories revolves around a conflict. Conflicts may be external, between the main character and another character (or force), or internal, in which the main character must come to terms with something. Identify both an external and an internal conflict in the plot of "The Kayak." How are these two conflicts related? Which do you think is more important? Why?

3. Often, fiction writers use details of setting to reflect or emphasize the main character's state of mind. Identify at least two place details in "The Kayak" that help convey a sense of Teresa's state of mind.

4. Most short stories are written from either a first-person point of view (I), or a third-person point of view (he/she). Why do you suppose Debbie Spring chose the first-person point of view to tell her story? What benefits can you see to this point of view? What limitations does it impose?

Note: For more on first- and third-person point of view, see Unit 5.

5. To help their readers "see" the story in their minds, writers often include physical details about their characters. Identify two passages in the story that provide details about a character's physical appearance. How is the author able to include these details without interrupting the action of her story?

6. Most short stories span a relatively brief time period, often beginning in the middle of the action and filling in necessary details as the story progresses. Find examples in the model to show how an author can include important details that happened before the story begins.

7. Short story writers usually prefer to show rather than tell what a character is like. Some techniques for revealing character include dialogue, the reactions of other characters, physical description, and the character's own words and actions. Which of these techniques does the author of the model story use? Give examples.

8. At the heart of every short story is its theme, an understanding about life that the writer wishes to share with the reader. The theme is usually closely tied to the change that occurs in the story. For example, the main character's situation or view may change, or the reader's opinion of the main character may change. Identify what changes during the

story "The Kayak" and explain what the writer shows us about life through this change.

Checkpoint: Short Story

 As a class, create a checklist of common features of short stories, based on what you have just learned. You can use the checklist to help you write your own short story.

Writer's Workshop

1. Decide whether your main character will be male or female and give this person a name. On a blank sheet of paper, make headings such as physical features, family members, friends, school, job, favourite things, dislikes, talents, hopes/dreams, fears, history, and any others you can think of. Then, list as many details under as many headings as possible. You will not use all these details in your story; the purpose of this exercise is to help you envision your character clearly.

2. Look over your list of details and decide whether you have enough information about this person to continue. One good test for this is to describe your character aloud to a classmate or friend and ask if your listener needs more information. Talk about your character freely and, as you think of more details, jot these down.

   Learning Goal
   - **write a short story**

3. The main character of every story wants something, whether an actual thing or something intangible. Read over your character details and decide what it is your main character wants; then identify what might keep your main character from getting it. Try to state this conflict in one or two sentences.

4. Now imagine a situation in which your main character comes into conflict with the person or force that is preventing her or him from getting what she or he wants. If possible, brainstorm several different situations and choose the one you find most interesting and believable for a reader.

5. Write a draft that describes the conflict you have created. Remember to begin the story somewhere in the middle, and work in necessary information as you write. To help you keep track of events, you may want to draw a time line of the events in the story.

 6. Revise your work using the list you created at Checkpoint. Try to limit the length of your revised draft to no more than three typed pages by omitting unnecessary information and focusing on conflict and character.

Oral Language Extension

Form a writers' group with three other classmates. Before your group meets, identify one or two concerns you have about your short story that you would like the group to address. The purpose of your meeting will be to identify ways to improve your story and to help others do the same. Since it can be intimidating at first to share your writing, work on creating an atmosphere of cooperation and trust in the group. Listen carefully and respectfully to other people's stories.

IDEA FILE

When working in a group, you need to know how to give constructive, as opposed to destructive, criticism. Here are some hints to help you phrase your comments in a positive way:

- Tell what you like as well as what you don't like.

- Be as specific as possible in your criticism. Avoid blanket statements such as "That's wrong" or "I don't like that."

- When you criticize, try to suggest ways to fix the problem at the same time.

- Preface your statements with words like "It seems to me that ..." or "I find that ..." or "Perhaps ..." rather than making flat statements.

- Be positive, but do not gloss over problems to spare someone's feelings.

Grammar

Nouns, verbs, adjectives, and adverbs are the most important parts of speech because we can write complete sentences using only them. However, the four other parts of speech also perform important functions that help to make sentences more varied and interesting. These parts of speech are pronouns, prepositions, conjunctions, and interjections.

> **Learning Goal**
>
> • use parts of speech correctly: pronouns, prepositions, conjunctions, and interjections

A **pronoun** is a word that takes the place of a noun.

I toss the rope. *He* misses. *I* throw *it* again and *he* catches *it*.

There are several different types of pronouns. They include the following:

- personal pronouns: *I, me, mine, you, your, yours, he, him, his, she, her, hers, it, its, we, our, ours, they, their, theirs*

- indefinite pronouns: *all, another, any, anybody, anyone, anything, both, each, either, every, everybody, everyone, everything, few, little, many, much, neither, nobody, none, no one, nothing, one, other, several, some, somebody, someone, something*

- reflexive pronouns: *myself, yourself, himself, herself, itself, ourselves, yourselves, themselves*

- relative pronouns: *who, whom, whose, which, that*

- demonstrative pronouns: *this, that, these, those*

- interrogative pronouns: *what, which, who, whom, whose*

Note: For more on pronouns, see Unit 12.

A **preposition** is a word that shows the relationship between a noun or pronoun and another word in the same sentence.

"He is trapped *underneath* the sail."

Some frequently used prepositions are *with, at, by, from, in, on, of, over, across, along, before, after, between,* and *through.*

Note: For more on prepositions, see Unit 3.

A **conjunction** is a joining word that connects words or groups of words.

Coordinating conjunctions join the same kinds of structures, such as nouns, verbs, sentences, and so on. The four most common coordinating conjunctions are *and, but, nor,* and *or.*

   Subordinating conjunctions join only clauses, and one of these clauses depends on the other.

   The waves peak wildly *as* the storm picks up.

Other subordinating conjunctions include *although, because, until, before, since, unless, until,* and *while.*

Note: For more on conjunctions, see Units 4 and 5.

An **interjection** is a word or group of words that shows strong feeling or emotion.

Examples of interjections are *hey, wow, huh,* and *gosh.*

1. Identify whether the boldface words are pronouns, prepositions, conjunctions, or interjections. Explain your choices.
   a) I approach Cousin Island, **where** I have to steer **around** the submerged rocks.
   b) **That**'s what you shout, **in** water skiing, **when** you're ready to take off.
   c) **It** will be slow **because** we're going **against** the current.
   d) I thought I was good **at** all water sports, **but** windsurfing sure isn't one of **them**.
   e) **Wow,** you gave me a heart attack until you flipped the kayak back over.

2. Some words can act as either prepositions or subordinating conjunctions, depending on their use in the sentence. Identify the part of speech of each boldface word and explain your choice.
   a) **After** the sail fell into the water, it was too heavy to lift.
   b) Teresa and Jamie went to a campfire **after** the storm.
   c) Teresa had not been asked out by a boy **until** that day.
   d) Jamie had no idea Teresa was paralyzed **until** he saw her wheelchair.

3. Working with a partner, list all the pronouns, prepositions, and conjunctions in the first three paragraphs of "The Kayak." Find one interjection later in the story.

MEDIA LINK

Plan a television dramatization of "The Kayak" aimed at a teen audience. In a small group, decide which actors you would choose for the lead roles. Would you use the same title? What time-slot would you use? Create a full-page print advertisement for this television drama. What other techniques would you use to publicize this made-for-television movie? Present your advertisement and publicity campaign to the class.

Mechanics

Dialogue is one of the most effective devices a writer can use to help readers visualize a story. It serves several functions:

- It offers variety by breaking up the narrative.
- It can help to advance the plot by providing opportunities for characters to come into conflict with each other.
- It reveals character through spoken comments and unique expressions.

Generally speaking, use quotation marks around the actual spoken words of a character, use a comma to separate a speech from a speaker tag (words that identify the speaker), begin each new speech with a capital letter, and place end punctuation inside the closing quotation marks.

"Hit it," the boy calls.

I said, "Next time, wear a life jacket."

Learning Goal

• punctuate and capitalize dialogue correctly

1. Read the following examples of dialogue, and identify how each one differs from the rule for punctuating dialogue given on the previous page. Write additional rules to explain each of the new examples. When you have finished, compare your rules with those of other classmates to make sure your list is accurate.

   a) "Can you get back to shore?" I ask.
   b) What do you mean by "Hit it"?
   c) "What you really want to know," I said, "is how long I've been crippled."
   d) "Drop the sail!" I call.
   e) What a surprise when he said, "I'll pick you up at nine"!

2. Use your rules to capitalize and punctuate the following passages of dialogue.
   a) there looks to be a storm coming up said teresa's father.
   b) i'll be careful on the lake she assured him.
   c) he asked do you want me to go out with you?
   d) dad teresa said you know i've kayaked in the rain before.
   e) i know you have he said it's just that the forecast is calling for wind.
   f) i'm sixteen years old teresa shouted i'm not a baby anymore!

Note: For more on punctuating quotations, see Unit 5.

WRITING TIP

To make your character's speech sound natural and realistic, listen to the way people actually speak. Use short sentences, sentence fragments **(see Unit 11)**, and words that your character would really use.

3. Read your short story and see if you have made use of opportunities to have characters speak aloud. If so, check that you have capitalized and punctuated your dialogue correctly. If not, look for passages where you can replace narration with dialogue.

Usage & Style

Professional writers understand that it's not fair to surprise a reader with an ending that does not grow out of the events of the story. For an ending to be believable, it must logically follow from what has gone before it. In "The Kayak," for example, the author prepares her readers for the surprise about Teresa's paralysis by including details early in the story that offer hints about her condition. This attempt to provide hints in a story about events to come is a literary device called **foreshadowing**.

1. Identify the foreshadowing offered in the first paragraph of the story. When you first read the story, you probably missed the significance of these lines. What do you understand them to mean now?

> ### Learning Goal
> - **identify elements of foreshadowing in short stories**

2. Find at least two other passages that foreshadow the moment when Teresa reveals her disability. How has your understanding of these passages changed since the first time you read the story?

3. In the sixth paragraph, Teresa watches a loon as it dives for a fish. Read this paragraph and explain how it foreshadows a later event.

4. In what way is the title of the story itself, and the situation portrayed, a foreshadowing of the ending? Discuss with a partner.

5. Read your own short story and decide whether you have prepared your reader for the ending. Do you need to include details earlier in your story that foreshadow your ending?

Word Study & Spelling

I notice a windsurfer with a flashy *neon* green and purple sail.

The word *neon* comes from the Greek word *neos*, meaning "new." It was given to a gas discovered by Sir William Ramsay and Morris William Travers in 1898, and eventually came to be used in coloured lighting. The word has developed a new meaning in recent times, referring to particularly bright fabric colours.

Just as colours continually change in the fashion industry, so do the meanings of words in the English language. Here are some ways that words change:

- **Generalization** occurs when a word takes on a broader meaning than it originally had; *pen* originally meant a writing implement made from a bird's feather, but it now refers to a variety of writing instruments.

- **Specialization** occurs when a word takes on a narrower meaning than it originally had; *meat* once referred to any kind of food but now refers only to animal flesh.

- **Elevation** occurs when the meaning of a word takes on a higher value; the word *angel* originally referred to a messenger but has been elevated to refer to a guardian spirit.

- **Degradation** occurs when the meaning of a word lessens in value: *vulgar* once meant "referring to common people," but now we understand it to mean "coarse" or "crude."

1. Identify whether the meaning of each of the following words has been generalized, specialized, elevated, or degraded. The original meaning of the word is given in parentheses.
   a) hound
      (any dog)
   b) smirk
      (a smile)
   c) awful
      (impressive)
   d) salary
      (money given to Roman soldiers to buy salt with)
   e) idiot
      (an uneducated person)
   f) thing
      (a matter brought before a court)
   g) fame
      (reputation)

WORD ORIGINS

The word *kayak* is one of many words that Canadian English has inherited from Inuktitut and the languages of Aboriginal peoples. In groups of three, find at least three other words that have entered the English language from an Aboriginal language. (HINT: Try *The Canadian Encyclopedia*.) Identify which particular Aboriginal group each word was borrowed from. What do you notice about the kinds of words that were adopted? Why do you think this is?

Looking Back

Before handing in your final edited draft, have a classmate check your short story, paying particular attention to the following:

- ☑ Has the author used dialogue to add variety, to advance the plot, and/or to reveal character?

- ☑ Is the dialogue punctuated and capitalized correctly?

- ☑ Is the ending foreshadowed effectively?

- ☑ Are all words spelled correctly?

Unit ③ Script

What is a script?

A script is a story told through the speech and actions of the characters involved. Besides including dialogue, the scriptwriter provides information about the setting and the characters' actions in brief stage directions.

Learning Goals

- write a scene for a script
- use prepositional and participial phrases correctly
- use punctuation in scripts correctly
- identify dialect
- avoid misplaced and dangling modifiers
- create personal and class dictionaries of newly encountered words

In this scene from a stage play, Tim has been laid off from his factory job and is working for Mrs. Phipps, a retired mathematics professor. When Tim's wife, Ginny, is offered a job in another city, all three characters are thrown into conflict.

Odd Jobs

BY FRANK MOHER

MRS. PHIPPS's yard. It has snowed; there is a dull, grey light. Some green garbage bags sit to one side. TIM is out sweeping the walk. MRS. PHIPPS enters, wearing her sweater. She stands watching. TIM spots her.

MRS. PHIPPS:	Your wife came to visit me yesterday.
TIM:	Yeah, I, uh, heard about that.
MRS. PHIPPS:	She told me you're not going to Regina.
TIM:	That's right.
MRS. PHIPPS:	That's true?
TIM:	Uh-huh. That is to say I'm not goin' yet.
MRS. PHIPPS:	I told her it was the silliest thing I'd ever heard.
TIM:	Well, yer entitled to your opinion.
MRS. PHIPPS:	She thinks so, too.
TIM:	Uh-huh. Well, that's what makes this country great.
MRS. PHIPPS:	Of course you're going to Regina. She's your wife, it's a good opportunity for her, you'll pack your tools and go.
TIM:	You through dictatin' my life for me, Mrs. Phipps?
MRS. PHIPPS:	Well, you're certainly not going to stay here!
TIM:	Look, if Ginny wants to go to Regina, that's all right with me. Regina will still be there, y' know, whenever. As for me, I got things to do here. Now, you gonna move off the sidewalk so's I can sweep it?

MRS. PHIPPS: I might.

TIM: You might. Well, I might just do it anyway. [*sweeping around MRS. PHIPPS*] Just leave it go, Mrs. Phipps, would you just leave it go? I got this walk to clean. I got weatherstrippin' to do. And that garage is a rat's nest. I haven't even begun to get 'er cleaned out.

> *Pause. TIM sweeps. MRS. PHIPPS glances over at the bags.*

MRS. PHIPPS: You never spread those leaves like I asked, did you?

TIM: No, I didn't.

MRS. PHIPPS: Well, there's no use now.

TIM: Well, I'll get to it later.

MRS. PHIPPS: No, there's no use now.

TIM: Mrs. Phipps, there's maybe one inch of snow here!

MRS. PHIPPS: And the painting in the basement. And the brown spots in the lawn. You haven't quite been keeping up here, have you?

TIM: Well, I got all winter, don't I?

MRS. PHIPPS: Not if it's forty below out.

TIM: Well, it's gonna be warm inside, isn't it?

MRS. PHIPPS: Not if you don't spread those leaves.

> *Pause.*

TIM: Mrs. Phipps, I know why you're doing this.

MRS. PHIPPS: Do you?

TIM: Yes.

MRS. PHIPPS: Well then?

TIM: The answer is no.

> *Pause.*

MRS. PHIPPS: Well then, I'll just have to do them myself. [*starting toward the bags*]

TIM: Mrs. Phipps, leave the bags.

MRS. PHIPPS: Seeing as you won't.

TIM: I told ya I'd do them.

MRS. PHIPPS: Seeing as it's October—

TIM: I'LL SPREAD THE LEAVES, ALL RIGHT MRS.
PHIPPS? HERE, I'M SPREADIN' THE LEAVES.
[*jumping on the pile of bags, ripping one open and
swinging it about*] HOW'S THAT? HUH? I'M
SPREADIN' THE LEAVES! MORE LEAVES? MORE
LEAVES! WHOOPEE! LET'S SPREAD THEM LEAVES!
HOWZAT? HUH? YOU THINK THAT'S ENOUGH?

               Pause.

MRS. PHIPPS: Yes. I think that will do.

TIM: Good. I'm glad you're happy.

MRS. PHIPPS: I guess this means you're fired.

TIM: I'm what?

MRS. PHIPPS: You're fired. Go on, get out of here.

               Pause.

TIM: You don't mean that, Mrs. Phipps.

MRS. PHIPPS: I certainly do.

TIM: Look, I'll clean up the leaves—

MRS. PHIPPS: WOULD YOU PLEASE GO AWAY.

Investigating the Model

1. Like short stories, scripts present characters in conflict. Identify the conflict established in this scene from *Odd Jobs* and explain whether it is internal or external.

2. The setting (time and place) of a dramatic scene, in addition to meeting the requirements of the plot, may set the mood or convey information about the characters and/or the theme. What significance can you see in Frank Moher's choice of setting?

3. Scriptwriters look for ways to enhance the dramatic value of a scene through the words of the characters (and their silences), through their actions on stage, and sometimes by making suggestions about how the scene should be presented. Such suggestions are usually included in stage directions. Note the information that is included in the stage directions for this scene from *Odd Jobs*. What sort of information has the playwright left out? Why do you think he chose not to include this information?

4. A scriptwriter carefully chooses words and expressions that convey a strong impression of the people speaking them. Give examples of dialogue in the model that give the audience insight into the people in this scene.

5. Often, what is not said by characters in a script is just as important as the words that are actually spoken. Suggest a comment that remains unspoken in *Odd Jobs*. Why do you think Frank Moher chose not to have this comment spoken aloud?

6. The saying "Actions speak louder than words" is especially true of scriptwriting. What actions performed by characters in the model convey a strong impression of the people and the conflict?

7. Every scene of a script, no matter how brief, should serve a particular purpose, whether to reveal information about a character or to advance the plot in some way. What purpose is achieved by the scene in the model?

Checkpoint: Script

 As a class, create a checklist of common features of scripts, based on what you have just learned. You can use the checklist to help you write your own script.

Writer's Workshop

1. Brainstorm a situation in which two characters might come into conflict. From your list, choose one situation that you think would make an interesting scene.

IDEA FILE

Here are some situation ideas to get you started:
- two athletes
- girl/boyfriend
- teenager/parent
- shoplifter/store owner
- speeding motorist/police officer
- bus driver/passenger
- mail carrier/dog owner
- waiter/customer

2. Jot down background information and details about the characters involved, focusing on what has led them to this situation. Remember, the better you know your characters, the more real they will seem to your readers.

3. Choose a setting in which your characters might come into conflict and that will immediately convey information about your characters to an audience. Visualize this setting and jot down details that will help a reader see the place as you do.

> **Learning Goal**
> - **write a scene for a script**

4. Because you will be writing a single scene rather than an entire script, you need not concern yourself with resolving the conflict between your characters. Instead, your purpose is to establish who your characters are and what conflict they are experiencing. With this in mind, plan the action of your scene.

5. Now consider the dialogue that will support and reflect the action in your scene. Picture the scene in your mind and imagine the conversation that takes place between your characters. Since your audience will not know who your characters are, part of the conversation will have to establish the previous history, or "backstory," that drives the action. Consider ways to work elements of this backstory into the scene.

6. Characters can reveal themselves through actions as well as dialogue, so try to think of what the actors will be doing while they are speaking.

7. Write a draft of the scene, remembering to include brief stage directions that will indicate pauses or show your reader what your characters are doing.

☑ 8. Read the scene aloud to get a sense of how it sounds. Make any changes you think are necessary. Then use the list you created at Checkpoint to revise your script.

Oral Language Extension

Playwrights will often "workshop" their plays before they are staged in front of a live audience. In an acting workshop, actors discuss the scene with the playwright, read the parts out loud, discuss changes, ask questions, and make suggestions to him or her. The playwright makes revisions based on their feedback and what he or she sees on stage.

1. a) In groups of three, take turns workshopping each other's script dialogues. Use the listening techniques outlined on page 205 to get the most out of the exercise. As an actor you should

- read the scene carefully before trying it out
- ask the author questions to clarify meaning or character
- be open to his or her directions
- make sure you understand the characters and the action
- make concrete, helpful suggestions

As a playwright you should

- answer the actors' questions
- be open to their interpretations

- attend carefully to how the script comes across on stage
- make revisions based on your own observations and the actors' suggestions

b) Afterward, evaluate how well you worked as a group. Did everyone get a chance to participate? Were people courteous and willing to listen to others' points of view? Were any conflicts handled well? Was the feedback you received useful? What could you do to improve the effectiveness of the group?

2. a) Once you have finalized the changes to your scripts, meet with the group members you workshopped with, and together choose one of your three scenes to present to the class. The playwright will act as director, and will introduce the performance to the class with a brief description of the title, background, and/or setting of the scene. The other group members will be actors.

b) Rehearse the scene several times, until the actors know the lines by heart, and the director is satisfied with the presentation. Consider using props or music to increase the effect of your performance.

c) After the performance ask for feedback from the class, and make note of their suggestions for improvement. Be prepared to offer advice and constructive suggestions to other groups as you watch their presentations.

Grammar

A **phrase** is a group of words that lacks a subject or a verb (or both) but functions as a unit within a sentence.

Sometimes, a group of words functions together as a single part of speech or sentence element. Phrases can function as nouns (e.g., *a dull, grey light*) or verbs (e.g., *would have gone*). There are also several types of phrases that can function as modifiers. They include prepositional and participial phrases.

A **participial phrase** is made up of a participle (the forms of a verb that usually end in *-ing, -ed, -en,* or *-t*), its object, and any modifiers. Participial phrases function as adjectives.

> **Learning Goal**
>
> - use prepositional and participial phrases correctly

Mrs Phipps enters, *wearing her sweater.*

The leaves *strewn across the stage* start to blow away.

Playwrights often use participial phrases alone in stage directions. Note, though, that you cannot use a participial phrase (or any other type of phrase) alone as a sentence in other forms of writing.

1. Find three examples of participial phrases used as stage directions in the model.

WRITING TIP

To avoid choppy writing, combine short, related sentences by making one a participial phrase and inserting it into the other.

Choppy: Tim waited for Mrs. Phipps to speak. He tried to ignore the sinking feeling in his stomach.

Revised: Waiting for Mrs. Phipps to speak, Tim tried to ignore the sinking feeling in his stomach.

A **prepositional phrase** begins with a preposition and ends with a noun or pronoun. Prepositional phrases can act as adjectives or adverbs.

Adjective phrase: Don't forget the painting *in the basement.*

Adverb phrase: Please move *off the sidewalk* so I can sweep it.

2. Identify the prepositional phrase in each of the following sentences and tell whether it is acting as an adjective or an adverb. (HINT: If the word the phrase is modifying is a verb, the prepositional phrase is acting as an adverb; if it is modifying a noun, the phrase is acting as an adjective.)
   a) She told me you're not going to Regina.
   b) Well, yer entitled to your opinion.
   c) She's your wife, it's a good opportunity for her.
   d) You haven't fixed the brown spots in the lawn.

3. Find at least one more prepositional phrase in the model. Copy the sentence in which it appears, underline the prepositional phrase, and draw an arrow from the phrase to the word it modifies. Then tell whether the phrase is acting as an adjective or an adverb.

MEDIA LINK

A storyboard is a series of drawings in frames (like a comic strip). Producers use storyboards when filming TV shows and films. Written below or beside each frame are the audio and the visual instructions to accompany each shot. Create a storyboard for the scene you wrote earlier in this unit. You may sketch your frames roughly, with stick figures, or complete them in full colour and great detail. Each frame should represent only a few seconds of screen time. Under each frame, write the dialogue, along with audio instructions for music and sound. Visual instructions should specify camera angles and distances (e.g., closeup, long shot).

Mechanics

Because scripts are meant to be read aloud, scriptwriters use a number of mechanical devices so readers will know how dialogue should sound when spoken.

> TIM: Now, you gonna move off the sidewalk so's I can sweep it?

In the passage above, Frank Moher uses nonstandard spelling ("gonna") and contractions ("so's") to help readers "hear" Tim's relaxed manner of speaking.

1. Find at least four other passages in the model that use contractions and/or nonstandard spelling to help readers hear the natural flow of a character's speech. Copy these and read them aloud to hear the effects of these devices.

Learning Goal
- **use punctuation in scripts correctly**

2. Scripts make use of other forms of punctuation as well. Read through the model script, as well as other scripts you find in the library or literature anthologies, and create a guide book for presenting scripts. In

your book identify the particular uses of the following punctuation marks and capitalization in scripts:

- capital letters
- square brackets
- long dash
- ellipsis
- colon
- italics

You could also include formatting tips for presenting different kinds of scripts (e.g., for radio, TV, and stage). When you have finished your guidebook, present a copy to the school library as a reference.

3. Listen carefully to a conversation, concentrating on the sound of the language used. Record at least three exchanges using nonstandard spelling, contractions, dashes, or ellipsis to capture the sound of the language.

Learning Goal

- **identify dialect**

4. Dialect is a term meaning the variety or form of a language that is characteristic of a particular group or geographical region. Working with a partner, select a novel that includes examples of the dialect of a particular region and rewrite a portion of a conversation in script form. Practise reading it aloud and then tape-record this conversation to share with the class. Include in your presentation a discussion of the various devices the writer used to help you "hear" and deliver the passage as it was intended.

Note: For information on slang and colloquialisms, see Unit 11.

IDEA FILE

Try the following books for examples of dialect:
- *Jake and the Kid* by W.O. Mitchell (the Prairies)
- *Hold Fast* by Kevin Major (Newfoundland)

5. Read your script and see if there are places where you could use the devices described in this lesson to convey the sound of your characters' language.

Usage & Style

To avoid dangling or misplaced modifiers, place modifiers, especially phrases, as close as possible to the words they modify.

Dangling modifiers occur if the word being modified does not actually appear in the sentence.

Dangling modifier:	*Ripping the bags open,* the leaves were scattered everywhere. (Did the leaves rip the bag?)
Corrected:	*Ripping the bags open,* Tim scattered the leaves everywhere.

> **Learning Goal**
> - avoid misplaced and dangling modifiers

The following passage contains a different problem:

Misplaced modifier:	*Piled by the walkway,* Mrs. Phipps tripped over the bags of leaves.
Corrected:	Mrs. Phipps tripped over the bags of leaves *piled by the walkway.*

When modifiers are placed too far away from the word they modify, confusion can result. Similar problems can occur when writers use prepositional phrases.

Misplaced modifier:	On the ceiling, Mrs. Phipps saw a spot that Tim had not painted.
Corrected:	Mrs Phipps saw a spot *on the ceiling* that Tim had not painted.

1. Rewrite the following stage directions, making changes that will correct any modifier problems. If a sentence contains no modifier problem, write Correct.
   a) Tim notices a broom working near the shed with a long handle.
   b) Tim starts to carry several cartons downstairs filled with math books.
   c) Working on several math equations in her office, the wind suddenly blows Mrs. Phipps's papers out the window.
   d) Wearing her sweater, Tim greets Mrs. Phipps in the yard.
   e) Tim sweeps the leaves with an angry look to one side.

2. Read your script and look for problems with modifier placement, especially in your stage directions.

Word Study & Spelling

WORD STUDY & SPELLING

Learning Goal

- **create a personal dictionary of newly encountered words**

Actors have to memorize their lines in a short amount of time. To help them, they often use memory tricks and word associations. Memory tricks and associations can also help you remember the spelling of troublesome words. Here are some techniques to help you remember difficult spellings.

- Use mnemonic devices: rhymes, puns, and word associations. For example, the words *dessert* and *desert* are often confused. Remember the difference in their spellings by saying "two servings for dessert" and "alone in the desert."

- Break compound words down into smaller words and pronounce both parts (e.g., *side-walk; weather-stripping*)

- Group together words that have similar patterns. Sometimes you can figure out how a word is spelled by relating it to a base word (e.g., *sweater—sweat*) or to another spelling pattern (e.g., *spreading—heading*).

- Consider word origins. Many English words have been borrowed from other languages with different spelling patterns. For example, some English words that end in *-us* or *-um* have irregular plural spellings because they follow the pattern of the original language—Latin—from which they came. Examples are *focus—foci; radius—radii;* and *medium—media.* Knowing this can help you when you meet a new word that you suspect might come from a similar background.

Note: For more spelling strategies, see Unit 6.

1. Use at least one of the strategies given here to suggest a way to remember the proper spelling of each of these words from the script.

   a) forty   **b)** weather   **c)** certainly

   d) spread   **e)** through   **f)** opportunity

2. **a)** Create a dictionary of words you have trouble spelling. Every time you notice a spelling mistake in your work, add it to your dictionary. Use one or more of the ideas given here to write a memorization strategy next to the word in your personal dictionary.

   b) Create a class dictionary of frequently misspelled words and display it in the classroom. Use it to have a spelling contest.

WORD ORIGINS

The great English playwright William Shakespeare was singlehandedly responsible for introducing many Greek and Latin words into English, including **accommodation, apostrophe, dislocate, frugal, obscene,** and **reliance.** In addition, many lines from his plays have found their way into the language as familiar expressions. Use a dictionary of quotations to find the origin of each of the following quotations from Shakespearean plays. Write the longer quotation from which each expression comes, as well as the name of the play, the act, and the scene. With a partner, discuss the meaning of each expression.

brave new world

a sea change

all that glisters (glitters) is not gold

the course of true love never did run smooth

What's in a name?

Looking Back

Before handing in your final edited draft, have a classmate check your script, paying particular attention to the following:

 Is the dialogue realistic?

 Is the script punctuated correctly and consistently?

✓ Are phrases that modify placed immediately before or after the words they are modifying?

✓ Are all words spelled correctly?

Reflect and Build on Your Learning

Reflecting on Narrative Writing Forms

1. Review the Learning Goals on page 17. Which goals do you think you have achieved most successfully? Which goals do you think will require you to do more work? Why?

2. This section covered three forms of narration. What other forms of narrative writing do you know? (You may wish to review the features of narration on page 16.) Choose one of them and describe its features to a partner, explaining *why* and *when* you would use it. Does your partner agree with your explanation? Would you change anything you've said because of his or her feedback? In what way?

Looking Over Narrative Writing Forms

1. Working with a small group, discuss what you know about humorous personal narratives, short stories, and scripts. To guide your discussion, create a chart that includes these three forms, as well as the additional form you chose for activity #2 above. Develop five criteria for comparing the forms. One criterion might be use of dialogue. Complete the chart to compare the four forms. Compare your chart with those of other groups. How would you modify your chart based on what they have included in theirs?

CRITERIA	PERSONAL NARRATIVE	SHORT STORY	SCRIPT	OTHER
Dialogue				

Using the Narrative Writing Forms

1. Think about a humorous event that you experienced in one of your classes in a lower grade. Record everything you remember about that event, and write a draft of a humorous personal narrative for the school newspaper, using as a guide the class checklist of features for this form. Have a classmate read your draft, also using the class checklist as a guide. Revise your personal narrative as needed, and have your classmate edit and proofread it carefully, especially for the checklist of items on page 31.

2. Working with a partner, write the script for a scene involving two imaginary and invisible beings who have just landed at a particular place in your community. Your script is meant for presentation to the class and inclusion in a class collection of scripts. Include the beings' comments on the setting and human actions that they observe. Feel free to invent words based on existing English words. Revise, edit, and proofread your script, using as guides the class checklist for scripts and the checklist on page 61. Present your script to the class, either directly or on audiotape.

3. Write a short essay on an element of one of your favourite short stories such as first- or third-person point of view or setting. How does the author use the element to affect you as the reader? Revise and edit your essay to make sure it has a main point, with connecting words to help unify the information and ideas you are presenting.

4. Working with a partner, compile four lists of common English words classified as *borrowed* (from other languages), *slang/invented, dialect,* and *acronyms.* Include about six words in each list and display them for the class on four separate pieces of chart paper. Explain to the class how the four categories are different and ask your classmates for additional examples.

5. Working with a small group, identify a short scene from the film of a Shakespearean play to make a comparison with the original version of the scene. To identify the scene you want to use, look at a videotape of the film, the published script for the film, and the original version by Shakespeare. Pay attention to the use of stage directions in the original and to the instructions in the film script for the use of elements such as camera angles and visual effects. Present your comparison to the class, making sure to include an accurate and carefully proofread glossary handout of all technical terms you refer to. If possible, show the class a videotape of the film scene.

Description

A description is a word picture. Descriptive writing involves selecting details and choosing words that create a single strong impression, much as a painter uses colour, technique, and perspective to create a work of art. Often, descriptive passages are found within a longer piece of writing, and the dominant impression they convey helps to establish a mood, reinforce a theme, or introduce a character. Whether the subject is something tangible like a person, place, or event, or more abstract, such as an idea or a feeling, the process of choosing details and presenting them in a purposeful way remains the same.

This section contains three forms of descriptive writing that stand on their own: poetry, profile, and event description. Each piece paints a vivid impression of its subject, helping us to experience some part of the world through the eyes of another.

Features of Description

- Descriptions focus on creating a single dominant impression of a person, place, event, feeling, or idea.
- Descriptive writers choose words, images, and details that appeal to more than one sense, and that reinforce the dominant impression they want to give their readers.
- Descriptive writing often uses figurative language techniques such as simile and metaphor.
- Descriptions may be organized in various ways: spatially, chronologically, thematically, or in whatever way best suits the topic and purpose.

Learning Goals

- use print and electronic sources to gather information and explore ideas for your written work

- identify and use literary and informational forms appropriately in writing a poem, a profile, and an event description

- use organizational techniques to present ideas and supporting details

- revise your written work independently and collaboratively

- edit and proofread to produce final drafts using correct grammar, spelling, and punctuation

- use knowledge of vocabulary and language conventions; for example, use subjects and predicates correctly

- develop listening, speaking, and media literacy skills

- read a variety of fiction and nonfiction, such as poetry, profile, and event description

- identify and understand the elements and style of a variety of fiction and nonfiction

Unit 4 Poetry

What is poetry?

There are so many different poetic forms that a single definition is impossible; in fact, Samuel Taylor Coleridge defined poetry simply as "the best words in their best order." Most people, however, would agree that poetry is compact writing that evokes a strong emotional response through the use of vivid sensory details.

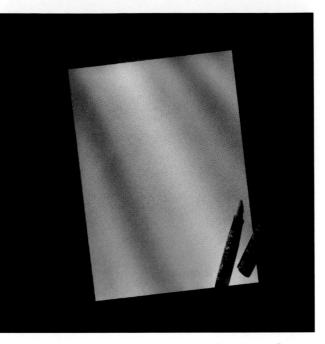

Learning Goals

- write a poem to explore your feelings
- use subjects and predicates correctly
- use main and subordinate clauses correctly
- adapt punctuation for poetry
- understand how authors use stylistic devices to achieve particular effects
- explore how prefixes affect the spelling of a word

Neither Out Far Nor In Deep

BY ROBERT FROST

The people along the sand
All turn and look one way.
They turn their back on the land.
They look at the sea all day.

As long as it takes to pass
A ship keeps raising its hull;
The wetter ground like glass
Reflects a standing gull.

The land may vary more;
But wherever the truth may be—
The water comes ashore,
And the people look at the sea.

They cannot look out far.
They cannot look in deep.
But when was that ever a bar
To any watch they keep?

Energy

BY LEONA GOM

One of the jobs
was putting up ice in winter,
cutting the big blocks from the dugout,
hauling them to the icehouse.
And then, that miraculous discovery
in burning July,
of the cold still crystallized
in the sawdust,
and me asking my father
why we couldn't save
pieces of heat from summer
the same way.
Him waving at the woodpile
he was building,
saying, there it is,
and it was one of those
epiphanies of childhood,
one of life's great harmonies understood,
and our place in it.

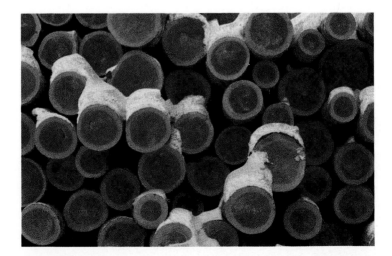

Fingerprints

**BY KIM JOHNSON
(16-YEAR-OLD STUDENT)**

When I tell you to sit down
you stand straight,
hands by your sides,
curled into small fists.
When I ask you to come with me,
you sit with thin arms
crossed defiantly.
You grin wildly when you are bad.
You are a disobedient child.
But you are not mine,
and I cannot stop you.
Insolent child.

Your arms are thin,
aren't they?
And bruised.
Has your defiance at home caused them
to pick you up
or drop you down?
Strange how there are always
four small bruises on the front,
a larger one on back.
Sometimes your cheek is—
Have you fallen off your bicycle?
        Again?
Poor child.

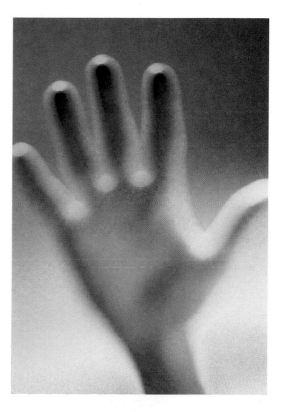

Investigating the Models

1. Unlike novels or short stories, which consist of a series of events leading to a resolution, poems often focus on a single moment. Write a sentence identifying the moment being described in each poem.

2. Successful poems evoke a strong emotional response in their readers. Choose one of the three poems and identify the response it evokes in you, explaining why the poem elicits this response.

3. List at least three questions you would like to ask one of the poets. Share your questions with other classmates who chose the same poem. Discuss possible answers for your questions. Are the answers to these questions important to your understanding of the poem? Why or why not?

4. Poets carefully select sensory details to convey a particular understanding or impression. Identify at least one sensory detail in each of the model poems that conveys a strong impression of the central experience being described.

5. Some poems, like "Neither Out Far Nor In Deep," follow a regular rhythmical pattern. What does this rhythm contribute to the theme of Frost's poem?

6. Free verse is poetry that does not follow a metrical pattern; instead, the poet tries to capture the flow of natural speech. Read "Energy" and "Fingerprints" aloud at least twice and compare the sound of these poems. Why do you think the poets chose to use free verse for their poems?

7. In "Neither Out Far Nor In Deep," Robert Frost uses a rhyming scheme in which the first and third lines rhyme and the second and fourth lines rhyme. What purpose does this rhyming pattern serve?

8. Poets break and skip lines in their poems to emphasize certain details or impressions. What details or impressions are heightened by the line breaks and spaces in the three poems?

9. Robert Frost once wrote, "Like a piece of ice on a hot stove the poem must ride on its own melting." Was he offering advice to poets or to readers? Choose one of the three poems and describe the "melting" process Frost was referring to.

Checkpoint: Poetry

 As a class, create a checklist of common features of poems, based on what you have just learned. You can use the checklist to help you create your own poem.

Writer's Workshop

1. Brainstorm a list of images or moments that seem particularly vivid in your memory. Consider moments when you experienced a strong emotion such as happiness, sorrow, fear, surprise, or excitement.

2. Put a check mark beside those images or moments that had the greatest impact upon you. From these, choose one you feel comfortable working with, and write a sentence or two identifying the importance this moment had for you.

> **Learning Goal**
>
> - **write a poem to explore your feelings**

3. Clear your mind and imagine yourself back in that moment. How do you feel? What do you see? hear? smell? taste?

4. Make a chart with the headings SIGHT, TOUCH, TASTE, SMELL, and HEARING, and jot down as many details about that moment as you can remember under each heading. You may not be able to record something under every heading, but try to include details that appeal to as many senses as possible.

5. From your chart, select the details you feel capture the emotion of that moment best. Use these details to write phrases or sentences (or both) that describe the experience. If possible, use comparisons that help show the experience clearly.

6. Because poetry is compact writing, see if you can use fewer words to say the same things. Specific nouns and verbs seldom require modifiers. You may want to use a thesaurus to help you find words that are appropriate for your purpose, but try to keep the poem sounding like you.

7. Arrange these phrases and sentences on the page in various ways, checking to see which arrangement conveys the most vivid impression of the moment you are writing about. Do you wish to follow a rhyming pattern, or is free verse better suited to your purpose?

TECHNO-TIP

It's easy to try different arrangements for your poem (e.g., line breaks, punctuation) if you are working on a computer. Save each version in a separate file so you can compare.

8. Refer back to the list you created at Checkpoint, and revise and edit your poem until you are satisfied with it. Give your poem a title.

Oral Language Extension

Reader's theatre is the dramatic presentation of a piece of writing through interpretive reading. Unlike performers in traditional theatre, reader's theatre performers stand or sit on the stage and focus on the oral delivery of their lines rather than on actions to evoke specific responses.

Working in a group of two or three students, select a poem—from an anthology, from those presented in this unit, or from those written by group members—that you think would appeal to your peers. Read the poem at least twice and share your responses, identifying the layers of meaning the poem suggests. Then, read it aloud several more times to get a sense of how the poem might be scripted to convey its central meaning, and prepare a reader's theatre presentation to deliver to the class. Use props, music, sound effects, or whatever else you think would enhance your reading. Rehearse the poem several times before presenting it. Be prepared to justify your treatment of the original poem and to assess the effectiveness of your classmates' presentations.

Grammar

All sentences have two main parts: a **subject** and a **predicate**.

Learning Goal

• **use subjects and predicates correctly**

The subject is the noun phrase that the sentence is about. The predicate is the verb phrase containing the action the subject is performing. Some verbs, however, are not action words, so the predicate may explain the condition or state of the subject.

The water **comes ashore.**
   subject   **predicate showing action**

Your arms **are thin,** aren't they?
   subject   **predicate explaining condition**

1. The simple subject is the most important word (noun or pronoun) in the subject, while the simple predicate is the most important word in the predicate (i.e., the verb). Identify the simple subject and simple predicate in each of the sample sentences above.

2. Find the complete subject and complete predicate in each of the following sentences. Then tell whether the predicate shows an action or explains a condition or effect.
   a) The people along the sand turn and look one way.
   b) They turn their back on the land.
   c) They look at the sea all day.
   d) One of the jobs was putting up ice in winter.
   e) It was one of those epiphanies of childhood.

> **WRITING TIP**
>
> For variety or emphasis, and to keep the reader's interest, writers often vary the position of the subject in a sentence.

The most basic sentence construction includes the subject immediately before the verb. Notice how Frost changes this structure somewhat in the following sentence.

The wetter ground like glass reflects a standing gull.

3. Find the simple subject and simple predicate in the sentence above. Rewrite the sentence so the verb immediately follows its subject. Which structure do you prefer? Why? Why do you think Frost used the structure above?

4. Notice how the subject-followed-by-verb structure changes when the sentence is written in question form. Identify the subject and predicate in each of the following. (HINT: Try saying the questions in statement form.)
   a) Has your defiance at home caused them to pick you up?
   b) Have you fallen off your bicycle?

5. Read your poem and check to see if you have varied the position of the subjects of your verbs. Decide if you need to make any changes.

Note: For more on sentence structure, see Units 5, 8, and 11.

A **clause** is a group of words that contains both a subject and a verb.

A **main clause** (or independent clause) makes a complete thought and can stand alone as a sentence. A **subordinate** (or dependent) **clause**, on the other hand, cannot stand alone as a sentence.

When I ask you to come with me, **you sit with thin arms crossed defiantly**.

subordinate clause   main clause

Learning Goal

• **use main and subordinate clauses correctly**

Subordinate clauses begin with **subordinating conjunctions** such as *although, because, before, since, unless, until, while, when, as, if, as if, who, which, that, after,* and *though.*

And, or, nor, for, but, so, and *yet* are **coordinating conjunctions**, which are used to join two main clauses together.

WRITING TIP

When combining subordinate and main clauses, keep the main action you want performed in the main clause.

Weak: **I tell you to sit down** *when you stand straight.*

main clause   subordinate clause

Better: *When I tell you to sit down,* **you stand straight**.

subordinate clause   main clause

6. Indicate whether each of the following is a phrase, a main clause, or a subordinate clause. Then tell how you know.
 a) the people along the sand
 b) they turn and look one way

  c) when the people look at the sea

  d) a ship keeps raising its hull

  e) as it begins to pass

  f) cutting the big blocks from the dugout

  g) him waving at the woodpile

  h) there are always four small bruises on the front

  i) you stand straight

  j) poor child

7. Read your poem and look for sentences in which you have combined main and subordinate clauses. If you have included any, make sure you have put the main actions in the main clauses.

MEDIA LINK

While a poem uses various techniques to create a "word picture," a music video uses visual hooks both to interpret the song and to promote the singers. In a small group, choose a music video and watch it three times, the second time without the soundtrack. List all the symbols that you see. Can you think of more than one way these symbols might be interpreted? Discuss how the artist or production company intended the video to be interpreted; then imagine individuals or groups that might interpret it differently. What interpretation did your group attribute to the video?

Mechanics

Everything in a poem should contribute to the overall emotional response the poet wishes to evoke. Even punctuation—or the lack of it—is often used to achieve this purpose.

  Most poetry is meant to be read aloud, so the poet uses periods and other forms of punctuation as well as line breaks and spaces to guide the reader in the oral interpretation of a poem. For example, a line break may signify a brief pause. A comma may extend the pause

> **Learning Goal**
>
> - **adapt punctuation for poetry**

slightly. Note the difference between the following passages when each is read aloud.

> The wetter ground like glass
> Reflects a standing gull.
>
> The water comes ashore,
> And the people look at the sea.

1. What does the extended pause in the second passage accomplish? Discuss with a partner.

2. Note the way Robert Frost punctuates the first two stanzas of "Neither Out Far Nor In Deep." Although the first two lines of each stanza are both complete thoughts, how does the end punctuation of the second line of each stanza differ? Why do you suppose Frost chose to punctuate these lines differently?

3. Note how the end punctuation of the second line of the third stanza in Frost's poem ("But wherever the truth may be—") differs from the second line of the first two stanzas. What purpose does this end punctuation serve? Suggest another form of punctuation that Frost might have used in its place, and copy the stanza using this form. Then read both your version and the original. Which do you prefer? Why?

4. The same form of punctuation identified in activity #3 above appears near the end of "Fingerprints." Does it serve the same function as in Frost's poem? Explain.

5. What form of punctuation in "Energy" does Leona Gom use more than any other? Read the poem aloud listening to the effect of these punctuation marks. Then read it aloud ignoring them. Did you have the same emotional response to the poem in this second reading? Explain.

6. Read your own poem aloud and look for places where you could use punctuation or line breaks to improve the poem or make it sound better when read aloud. Make these changes and then give your poem to someone else to read aloud. See if they read it as you intend or if you need to make further changes.

WRITING TIP

Remember that too many punctuation marks in a short poem can make it hard to read and, therefore, can hinder a reader's understanding and appreciation of the poem.

Usage & Style

Because poems are much shorter than most other forms of writing, poets must convey vivid impressions using as few words as possible. To accomplish this, they write figuratively, using language that suggests more than it states. For example, an effective way to describe something is to compare it to something else. Read the following passage from "Energy" and note how Gom conveys the breathless heat of summer in only two words.

> And then, that miraculous discovery
> in burning July ...

Learning Goal

- explain how authors use stylistic devices to achieve particular effects

Figurative comparisons show relationships between things that are unlike in nature. Here are five types of comparisons often used by poets and other writers.

- **Simile** is a direct comparison using *like* or *as.*

- **Metaphor** is an implied comparison. The phrase "burning July" is a metaphor because it compares the heat of summer to something on fire without using *like* or *as.* Metaphor can be especially effective in painting vivid sensory impressions because it requires readers to participate in making the comparison by mentally associating one image with another. For example, "The gulls stitched through the waves" uses a single verb to paint a mental picture of the seabirds' movement by calling to mind a needle passing through cloth. In this case, the suggestion of this motion is more effective than a simile such as "The gulls moved like needles through the waves."

- **Personification** is a special kind of comparison in which an animal, inanimate object, or an idea is given human qualities. "Death came knocking at my door" personifies death in this way.

- An **oxymoron** is a figure of speech that places opposites together to create a paradox. For example, *a thunderous silence, make haste slowly, fiery ice.*

- A **symbol** is an act or thing that represents more than itself. For example, Kim Johnson uses the marks on the child's body, "four small bruises on the front, / a larger one on back," as visual symbols of the violence the child experiences at home and, to a greater extent, domestic violence in modern society. Whereas simile, metaphor, and personification are comparisons drawn by the writer, the meaning of a symbol arises from the readers' experience, each reader drawing whatever connections are meaningful for her or him.

1. Identify the simile in "Neither Out Far Nor In Deep." Is this an effective comparison? Tell why or why not.

2. Identify at least one other metaphor in the poem "Energy," and explain the comparison Gom is suggesting.

3. In small groups, brainstorm a list of words and phrases you associate with the sea. Share your ideas with the class, and make a class list containing all your ideas. Now look at the Robert Frost poem, "Neither Out Far Nor In Deep." Which of your ideas would fit in with the sense of the sea in that poem? Meet with your small group again to discuss what you think the sea symbolizes in the process.

4. Look through a collection of poems in your local or school library to find at least one example of personification in a poem. Share your finding with the class.

Poets also use figurative language that appeals to sound.

- **Onomatopoeia** is the use of words that imitate sounds. *Screech* and *squawk*—sounds associated with seagulls—are onomatopoeic words.

- **Alliteration** is the repeated use of words that begin with similar sounds. Repeated soft sounds like "l" or "m" can create a feeling of peace and tranquillity (e.g., "the **l**ight **l**apping of the waves"), while repeated hard sounds like "k" or "t" can emphasize action and excitement (e.g., "the **c**uts and **c**ries of battle").

5. **a)** Make a list of onomatopoeic words that could have been used in one of the three model poems. Compare your list with that of a partner, and discuss which words you feel would be most effective in the poems.

   b) Identify examples of alliteration used in all three poems. Which example do you feel is most effective? Why?

6. Read your own poem again and identify places where you could paint vivid sensory impressions by using the figurative language techniques discussed here.

Word Study & Spelling

A **prefix** is a word part added to the beginning of a word to change its meaning.

Note: For information on suffixes, see Unit 5.

1. Find five different prefixes in the model poems. For each prefix, list at least two other words to which the prefix can be added. What happens to the meaning of a root word when these prefixes are added to it?

2. The prefix *dis-* appears in two words in the models. Find both words, and compare the meaning that is added to each base word. Is it the same? Why or why not? Think of at least two other words that use the prefix *dis-*, and identify the meaning of the prefix.

   Learning Goal
   - **explore how prefixes affect the spelling of a word**

3. *Insolent* begins with the Latin prefix *in-*. This prefix changes its spelling to *im-* or *il-* before some letters. With a partner, think of as many words as you can with *in-*, *im-*, or *il-* prefixes. Try to discover a rule that tells when to use *im-* or *il-* in place of *in-*. Prepare a chart explaining your rule.

4. The word *defiance* begins with the prefix *de-*, but these letters are part of the base word, not part of a prefix. With a partner, brainstorm a list of other words that look as if they begin with a prefix, but don't. Use a dictionary to help you.

WORD ORIGINS

and it was one of those
epiphanies of childhood ...
—Leona Gom

Epiphany comes from the Greek words *epi*, meaning "to," and *phainein*, meaning "to show." Traditionally, Epiphany is a Christian religious festival celebrating Christ's appearance to the wise men. Irish author James Joyce introduced the term into literary usage in the novel *A Portrait of the Artist As a Young Man*. He used it to describe a sudden "revelation of the whatness of a thing," more commonly understood to be a recognition of its inner truth.

The prefix *epi-* can have other meanings. Find three other words in the dictionary that contain the prefix *epi-*, and record the meaning of the prefix and the words.

5. Sometimes, it is hard to tell whether a word begins with an *in-*, *en-*, *em-*, or *im-* prefix. Read through the following groups of words, and choose the correct spelling. Then use the correct word in a sentence.
   a) incur, encur
   b) embassy, imbassy
   c) inpact, impact
   d) enpire, empire, impire
   e) enbody, embody, imbody
   f) inplant, implant
   g) enbroider, embroider, imbroider
   h) indulge, endulge
   i) install, enstall
   j) enbarrass, embarrass, imbarrass
   k) inportant, emportant, important
   l) inpulse, impulse
   m) inbankment, enbankment, embankment
   n) inpaired, empaired, impaired
   o) inpostor, enpostor, impostor
   p) enploy, employ, imploy

q) inply, emply, imply

r) inperial, imperial

6. Find two other prefixes that might be easily confused, and create a list of words like the one in activity #5 using these prefixes. Exchange your list with that of a classmate, and see how many words you each get right.

Looking Back

Before handing in your final edited draft, have a classmate check your poem, paying particular attention to the following:

 Has the poet varied the subject-predicate pattern in his or her sentences?

 Are main ideas expressed in independent clauses?

 Does the punctuation reflect the meaning of the poem and/or help the reader to recite it?

 Has the poet used figurative language effectively?

 Are all words, especially those with prefixes, spelled correctly?

Unit 5 Profile

What is a profile?

A profile is a short biography of an interesting person. Just as a drawn profile focuses on a single feature (the shape of a person's face), a written profile usually focuses on a single aspect of a person's background or experience that will be of interest to readers. The following newspaper article describes teenager Sean Knight's meteoric rise in the world of competitive in-line skating.

Learning Goals

- write a profile
- construct simple, compound, and complex sentences
- use ellipses and square brackets in direct quotations
- select first or third person to suit the form, purpose, and audience
- expand vocabulary by using suffixes

Guelph Teen Makes Mark on In-Line Skating Circuit

BY VALERIE HILL

AT 16 YEARS OF AGE, THE LANKY AND ATHLETIC SEAN KNIGHT tends to attract a lot of attention, particularly after leaping onto a narrow, metal hand railing on his in-line skates and sliding several metres before making a perfect landing. Defying gravity and every other law known to physics, the Guelph teen is a champion "aggressive skater," a term describing the high level of skill necessary to perform numerous mind-boggling tricks while spinning along on eight little plastic wheels. He currently holds a 12th-place ranking in Canada—not bad for a kid who started skating less than three years ago.

"A couple of friends were skating and I thought it was fun," he says. "First, I started jumping curbs." His next step was finding more challenging obstacles, such as the railings in front of a nearby townhouse complex. Neighbours, rather than complaining about Knight and his friends, view the sport as wonderful entertainment. "They come out to watch us.... They offer us drinks and stuff," says the grade 12 Guelph Collegiate student.

With few places to learn the skills and no coach available, Knight turned to skating videos, carefully watching the pros in action, then trying to copy their moves. "You see something and if you have the guts, you try it," he says. Watching the pros through the critical eye of a learner, the teen was deeply impressed by their abilities. "It's like they have no feeling in their bodies. It seems like it just comes to them and they never fall." Now, of course, he knows better and realizes the amount of work necessary to reach that level, not to mention the prerequisite number of bumps and bruises. He's also learned about the importance of quality skates, which are shaped similar to a downhill ski boot but come equipped with shocks in the heel area. They can easily run up to $400. Even the wheels—which must be changed frequently—cost about $80 per set. "They wear down and get lopsided," he says.

Unlike most other sports, in-line skating is based on freestyle moves, where skaters choreograph what they think will impress the judges. There are, however, some standard jumps, most sporting names like alley oop, fishbrain, fakil 720, true spin alley oop, mitsu, and grind (riding a metal rail).

When Knight had enough confidence and ability, he temporarily left the neighbourhood streets and began skating at Kitchener Bowl. Then he moved on to Rampage in Toronto, where most of the competitions are held. Last year was his first as a competitive skater, starting with events held by the skating clubs, then moving on to the more difficult Canadian Aggressive Tour that made stops across the country, including the Rampage club. "I came in 13 out of 25.... That was my first year," he says.

This summer, the Canadian Nationals came to Toronto and he was able to place in the top five during a qualifier on the previous weekend. When the main event rolled around, he was shocked to learn the judges had bumped him up to the expert class, instead of intermediate. Suddenly he was faced with skating against the top performers he'd seen on all those videos. "I loved it," he admits. "All the pros were there. We got to talk to them." He also got to beat a few. Knight placed 12th, barely missing out on a chance to move on to appear at the international competition in the United States. "The top 10 advanced and went on to Las Vegas," he says.

Competitions in aggressive skating are enough to give any parent nightmares. The kids must perform their own routines, skating in a sprawling course full of ramps, rails, and even pyramids. Judges are looking for speed, control, and—above all—level of difficulty, particularly in the height gained during a jump. One of Knight's favourite moves involves rolling up a "launch" ramp backward, completing two spins in mid air, then landing, preferably upright. As for his parents, "they support me big time," says the highly personable youth. His mother, however, had a hard time watching her son perform some of the more dangerous stunts. "She freaked out," he admits. His parents also relinquished most of their garage to accommodate a six-metre ramp, and their rec-room where an eight-centimetre pipe propped up on wooden supports cuts through the centre.

Next summer, Knight plans on attending Camp Woodward in Pennsylvania—the largest of its kind in the world. The camp recruits the best in the sport in all three disciplines: in-line skating, BMX bicycling, and skateboarding. As winter closes in and he's forced to give up outdoor skating, Knight and his pals—they call themselves the 519 Crew—will keep practising, using an indoor ramp they built together this summer from plans found on the Internet. At home, he'll work out on weights and use a trampoline to practise spins.

With such a promising start, by next summer, he might just make it to the top. ■

Investigating the Model

1. A profile often begins with a scene or action that establishes the identity and uniqueness of the subject. What significant details about Sean Knight does the first paragraph of the model reveal?

2. A profile usually focuses on a single experience or quality that makes the subject unique or intriguing. Explain whether or not you think the model succeeds in focusing on a single aspect of Sean Knight's experience.

3. Profiles may be arranged in a number of ways, depending on the focus of interest. For example, information may be presented in chronological (time) order, or each new section may focus on a new idea or a different characteristic of the person being profiled. What method of arrangement is used in the model? Why is this method appropriate to the topic? What other features of her subject might Valerie Hill have focused on?

4. A profile often includes physical descriptions of its subject that reinforce a particular impression of the subject that the author wants to convey. What characteristics of Sean Knight does Hill convey through her physical description?

5. A profile may include comments made by the subject or by other people about the subject. What do the quotations from Sean himself reveal about his personality? Suggest other people Hill might have

interviewed in writing the profile. Overall, what do you think quotations add to the style and content of a profile such as this one?

6. A profile often ends with a personal reflection made by the writer about the subject. Comment on the effectiveness of the model's conclusion.

Checkpoint: Profile

✓ As a class, create a checklist of common features of profiles, based on what you have just learned. You can use the checklist to help you create your own profile of someone.

Writer's Workshop

1. Brainstorm a list of people in your school or community whom you find interesting, either because they possess a unique quality or ability or because they have had an interesting experience. Choose one person from your list and ask him or her for permission to write a profile.

Learning Goal

• **write a profile**

2. In a sentence or two, identify the particular quality, ability, or experience that makes this person interesting. Jot down everything you know about this aspect of his or her life or personality.

3. Brainstorm at least five questions you would like to have answered about this person and arrange to interview the person you are writing about. You may also want to interview someone else who knows your subject well.

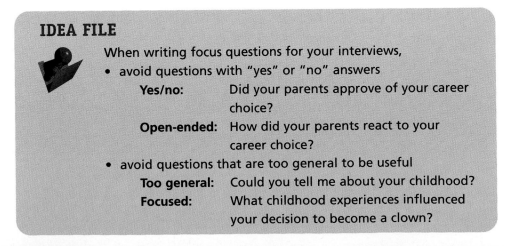

IDEA FILE

When writing focus questions for your interviews,
• avoid questions with "yes" or "no" answers

| **Yes/no:** | Did your parents approve of your career choice? |
| **Open-ended:** | How did your parents react to your career choice? |

• avoid questions that are too general to be useful

| **Too general:** | Could you tell me about your childhood? |
| **Focused:** | What childhood experiences influenced your decision to become a clown? |

4. If possible, use a tape recorder to record answers to your questions, in addition to writing them down. When you replay the interview, listen for comments that would be interesting to include in your profile.

5. Decide on an effective way to organize your information, and write a draft of your profile. Be sure to insert background details necessary for a reader who may not know your subject.

☑ 6. Refer back to the list you created at Checkpoint, and revise and edit your profile until you are satisfied with its focus, content, and organization.

Oral Language Extension

Re-enact *Front Page Challenge:*

1. With a partner, choose an individual who will be familiar to other members of the class and do some research about that person's life and accomplishments. He or she could be a political figure, an artist or writer, or even a member of your school community whom everyone would recognize.

2. One of you will be playing the role of this mystery guest, while the other will act as moderator. A panel of four other students will have five minutes to discover the identity of the guest by asking him or her yes or no questions. Panel members may consult amongst each other about what questions to ask. The moderator will keep track of whose turn it is to ask a question, watch the time, and clarify questions or answers, if necessary.

3. When five minutes are up, it is time for another pair from the group to act as moderator and mystery guest.

Grammar

Simple sentences contain only one subject and one predicate.

"I loved it.... All the pros were there. We got to talk to them."

Learning Goal

- construct simple, compound, and complex sentences

To find the subject, ask whom or what the sentence is about. To find the predicate, ask yourself what the subject is doing or what the sentence is telling us about the subject.

Note: For more on subjects and predicates, see Units 4 and 9.

> **WRITING TIP**
>
> Writers add variety to their writing by varying the length and the structure of their sentences. Although the three simple sentences on page 87 reflect natural speech, too many of them can make writing sound stilted and awkward.

1. Not all simple sentences are short. Identify the simple subject and simple predicate in each of the following simple sentences.
   a) At 16 years of age, the lanky and athletic Sean Knight tends to attract a lot of attention, particularly after leaping onto a narrow, metal hand railing on his in-line skates, sliding several metres before making a perfect landing.
   b) Defying gravity and every other law known to physics, the Guelph teen is a champion "aggressive skater," a term describing the high level of skill necessary to perform numerous mind-boggling tricks while spinning along on eight little plastic wheels.
   c) With few places to learn the skills and no coach available, Knight turned to skating videos, carefully watching the pros in action, then trying to copy their moves.

2. Look closely at the sentence parts you did not highlight in activity #1. What kind of grammatical constructions are they (e.g., phrases, clauses)? What do they add to the sentence?

3. Copy two more simple sentences from the model, one short and one long. Identify the simple subject and simple predicate in each.

> A **compound sentence** is formed when two main clauses are joined by a coordinating conjunction (*and, or, nor, for, but, so, yet*).

A couple of friends were skating   **and**   I thought it was fun.

     main clause   **coordinating conjunction**   main clause

Note: For more on subordinate and coordinating conjunctions, see Unit 2.

> A **complex sentence** consists of a main clause and one or more subordinate clauses.

Subordinate clauses can go before, after, or even in the middle of the main clause. If the main clause comes first, you do not usually need a comma; otherwise, separate the two clauses with commas.

You try it *If you have the guts*
main clause   *subordinate clause*

When Knight had enough confidence and ability, **he temporarily left the neighbourhood streets.**
   subordinate clause   **main clause**

Even the wheels, *which must be changed frequently,* **cost about $80 per set.**
   main clause   *subordinate clause*

4. Indicate whether each of the following sentences is simple, compound, or complex. Explain your answer.
   a) His next step was finding more challenging obstacles, such as the railings in front of a nearby townhouse complex.
   b) When the main event rolled around, the judges bumped him up to the expert class, instead of intermediate.
   c) It just comes to them and they never fall.
   d) He was faced with skating against the top performers whom he'd seen on all those videos.
   e) Neighbours, rather than complaining about Knight and his friends, view the sport as wonderful entertainment.
   f) The wheels on in-line skates wear down and get lopsided.
   g) As winter closes in, he's forced to give up outdoor skating.

5. Combine each of the following pairs of sentences, rewriting them first as a compound sentence and then as a complex sentence. Read both combined sentences aloud and tell which one you prefer and why.
   a) They come out to watch us. They offer us drinks and stuff.
   b) Sean watched the pros through the critical eye of a learner. He was deeply impressed by their abilities.
   c) Sean realizes the amount of work necessary to reach each higher level. He has also learned about the importance of quality skates.

d) This summer, the Canadian Nationals came to Toronto. Sean was able to place in the top five during a qualifier on the previous weekend.

6. Read a portion of your profile that is about 10 sentences long. Have you varied the length and structure of your sentences? If not, rewrite the passage making use of all three types of sentences. Try to vary the length of your sentences, too. Then, read each passage aloud. Which do you prefer?

MEDIA LINK

Watch a three- to five-minute videoclip of a fast-paced sporting event at least three times, the second time without the sound. Analyze the use of visual techniques (camera distance and angles, lighting, cuts, replays, slow motion) and the sound effects (voice-over, dialogue, sound, music, pace, and volume). Based on your analysis, what image is created of the "pros in action" in this clip? How realistic is this representation of the sport? How is the experience of watching this event on television different from actually being there?

Mechanics

Learning Goal

- use ellipses and square brackets in direct quotations

One of the best ways to create a strong impression of a person in writing—whether a fictional character or a real person—is to include the person's own words, or comments made about the person by others.

Pay attention to the following rules of punctuation when using quotations.

Note: For more on punctuating dialogue, see Unit 2.

Mark an **ellipsis** with three dots (...). When an ellipsis comes at the end of a quoted sentence, a fourth dot is needed to indicate the period.

Ellipsis is a term meaning "the omission of words or sentences from a quotation."

"I came in 13 out of 25.... That was my first year," he says.

1. Suggest a reason for the omission in the passage above. What might the author of the profile have left out?

2. Read through the quoted comments you may have included in your own profile. Are there places where you could use an ellipsis to omit unnecessary words or sentences that interrupt the flow of your writing?

> Use **square brackets** [ ] to insert words into a direct quotation.

Occasionally, you may need to insert words into a quotation so your reader understands what the speaker is saying. Set these words apart from the quotation by enclosing them in square brackets.

> "Then he moved on to Rampage [the Rampage Skate Club] in Toronto."

> "It's like they [the pros] have no feeling in their bodies."

> "They call themselves the [area code] 519 Crew," Hill reports.

3. Read the passages you have quoted in your profile and make sure the meaning of each word is clear. If not, insert necessary information using square brackets.

WRITING TIP

Speaker tags (e.g., *she said, he said*) are a good place to work in some interesting details about your subject. However, be careful not to include too many speaker tags, or your writing may start to sound stilted.

"They offer us drinks and stuff," *says the grade 12 Guelph Collegiate student.*

                                                       speaker tag

> Use both ellipsis points and square brackets as needed to integrate a quotation into your writing.

You can alter quoted material to make it fit into your writing, as long as you do not change the meaning of the original words, and as long as you indicate omissions or additions using ellipsis points and square brackets. Compare the following sentences with the original words used in the model.

> The article claims that "neighbours ... view the sport as wonderful entertainment."

> The writer explained that Sean's brand of skating "is based on freestyle moves [but that] ... there are ... some standard jumps."

4. Check the following passages against the words in the model and rewrite them, adding quotation marks, ellipsis points, and square brackets where they are needed.

   a) Valerie Hill describes in-line skates as being shaped similar to a downhill ski boot but with shocks in the heel area.

   b) The skates can easily run up to $400, and wheels cost about $80 per set.

   c) Judges, according to Hill, are looking above all for level of difficulty, particularly the height gained during a jump.

   d) Hill concludes by announcing Sean's plans for the future: Next summer, Knight plans on attending Camp Woodward, which recruits the best in the sport in in-line skating.

Usage & Style

Use **first-person point of view** to emphasize your own personal impressions of your subject.

Use **third-person point of view** to direct the reader's attention to the subject.

Learning Goal

- **select first or third person to suit the form, purpose, and audience**

Like most reporters, Valerie Hill chose to write her profile from an objective, third-person point of view. However, profiles can be, and often are, written in the first person. Hill could have used descriptions like those on the following page to convey her own impressions of Sean Knight:

I asked Sean what the neighbours thought of him practising on their railings ...

As I watch, Sean seems to defy gravity, and every other law known to physics.

Sean strikes me as a poised and confident young man ...

1. With a partner, try rewriting the first paragraph of the model including a first-person point of view. Discuss the advantages and disadvantages of each approach.

2. Although she uses the third person, Valerie Hill still manages to convey her opinion of her subject by choosing her words carefully. Read the following passages and pick out words that you think convey the writer's own impressions.

   a) At 16 years of age, the lanky and athletic Sean Knight tends to attract a lot of attention, particularly after leaping onto a narrow, metal hand railing on his in-line skates, sliding several metres before making a perfect landing.

   b) He currently holds a 12th-place ranking in Canada—not bad for a kid who started skating less than three years ago.

   c) With such a promising start, by next summer he might just make it to the top.

3. Read through your profile and identify the point of view you have chosen. Look for any places where your perspective has shifted from objective (third person) to subjective (first person). Also look for personal comments you may have made about your subject that might distract a reader. Decide whether you need to delete or revise them.

Word Study & Spelling

A **suffix** is a letter or group of letters added to the end of a word.

Note: For information on prefixes, see Unit 4.

1. a) Identify the root and the part of speech of each of the boldface words in the following examples. You may wish to use a dictionary.

Then Sean moved on to Rampage in Toronto, where most of the **competitions** are held.

Last year was his first as a **competitive** skater.

He **competed** against skaters with much more experience.

b) List at least two other words that have the same suffixes as the boldface words and use them in sentences. Do they function as the same part of speech as the words *competition, competed,* and *competitive* do in the examples above? Explain.

Learning Goal

• **expand vocabulary by using suffixes**

2. Adding a suffix can affect the function of a word. For example, the suffix *-tion* can turn a verb into a noun (attend + tion = attention). Find at least one suffix that fits each of the following criteria, and give an example of each. The first one has been done for you.

a) a suffix that makes a verb into a noun: **-er   teach + er = teacher**
b) a suffix that makes a verb change its tense
c) a suffix that makes a verb into an adjective
d) a suffix that makes an adjective comparative
e) a suffix that makes an adjective superlative
f) a suffix that makes an adjective into an adverb
g) a suffix that makes a noun or adjective into a verb

3. Compare your answers in activity #2 with those of your classmates, and create a class chart showing words with the same suffixes. Looking at the chart, what generalizations can you make about what words change their spelling when a suffix is added?

4. Below are more words from the model that have suffixes. Write the root of each word. Do any of these words follow the same generalization you arrived at in activity #2?
a) athletic
b) temporarily
c) aggressive
d) wonderful
e) entertainment

WORD ORIGINS

"Skate" comes from a Dutch word, *schaats.* It is also related to the Old French word for "stilts," *éschasse.* Skates, like stilts, give the wearer a longer stride.

Look up the word origins of these sports terms:

ski   golf   marathon   soccer

Looking Back

Before handing in your final edited draft, have a classmate check your profile, paying particular attention to the following:

☑ Is a variety of sentence lengths and structures used?

☑ Is quoted material smoothly integrated?

☑ Are ellipses and square brackets used properly in quotations?

☑ Is the point of view consistent and appropriate to the topic?

☑ Are all words, especially those with suffixes, spelled correctly?

Unit 6 Event Description

What is an event description?

An event description uses facts along with descriptive details (for example, what a scene looked like, how it felt to be there) to create an impression of what made the event memorable. The following model, from *Canadian Geographic* magazine, deals with an ice storm that crippled Eastern Canada in January of 1998.

Struck Powerless

BY ERIC HARRIS

IT WAS A SPECTACLE OF NATURE'S PREROGATIVE, A combination of meteorological forces that imposed an extraordinary burden of ice on a landscape accustomed to icy burdens. Persisting for six days, the ice storm that hit parts of Quebec and Ontario in January of 1998 was dubbed by some "The Storm of the Millennium." It was, indisputably, the storm of the century.

The rains came, unseasonably, from the deep south, a probable influence of El Niño, that periodic disruption of Pacific Ocean currents. The warm, wet weather reached the St. Lawrence River Valley late on

Sunday, January 4, and encountered an east-west front of southbound cold, dry air from northern Quebec. A stalemate ensued, with warm air above and cool air below—a textbook formula for freezing rain: snow from the upper reaches of the warm air turned to rain as it fell, the rain was super-cooled as it fell through the cold air below and froze as it hit cold surfaces. An atmospheric Zamboni, the storm flooded a rink greater than the Great Lakes with more than 80 millimetres of ice rain over six days. A frozen strata thick as pavement covered the country.

Collapse. Tracts of green ash and cedar, white pine and willow splintered violently under loads 30 times their own weight. Waist-thick limbs on century-old heirlooms snapped and snagged wires on city avenues. Poles down outnumbered those still up in some areas. Transmission towers crumpled like exhausted marathon runners near Saint-Hyacinthe, Que., and Cornwall, Ont.

Unfamiliar sounds and sights occurred each day: the glassy crashing of ice falling from trees distant and near; the unceasing rumble of generators reverberating across the countryside; the convoys of hydro, military, and phone crews on roadsides like liberation forces; the utter darkness.

The heroes: the Hydro-Québec linemen who risked all by dangling from a helicopter to refit a high-tension cable to a tower; the broadcasters on CBC Radio who unhaltingly fed the airwaves with reports on damage, repairs, relief, and weather; the neighbours who hauled generators house-to-house pumping sumps; the soldiers who carried seniors from frigid residences to shelters; the countless volunteers who fed and comforted the homeless thousands.

The villains: the man who went to Home Depot for a generator and left with a chain-cutter to obtain one by stealth; the thieves who took generators from houses while people slept, from telephone switchboxes, from railway crossings; the price-gougers.

The victims: 25 who died in Quebec and Ontario in a two-week aftermath, including Roland Parent of Sainte-Angélique, Que; who died of carbon monoxide poisoning; Ernest Jubien and Ethel Cockell-Jubien of Mont-Royal, Que; who died in a fire caused by a candle; Margaret Heath of Pierrefonds, Que., who died of hypothermia; Noella Cliche of Saint-Martin, Que; who died after being crushed by ice.

The toll was immeasurable. The single-minded *Financial Post* estimated damage at $500 million and losses from interrupted production at billions. Dairy farmers, apple growers, and sugarbush owners struggled to quantify their losses. Speculation swirled about hydro-electric rate increases as the utilities poured manpower and matériel into the fray. Property owners and municipal workers alike braced for a marathon of pruning.

Everyone had defining moments to recall, heart-rending or humanitarian. The view through my window at 6 a.m. on January 8 was an icon of the rural disaster zone. The hydro pole leaned at a 70-degree angle and the ice-encased wires dangled to the ground. Every tree, and there are hundreds, was snapped at the crown, cracked at major limbs, or bent over with tips frozen into the shining ground. A 12-metre green ash, the focal point of our front yard, lay cloven down the trunk. Half had fallen toward the road, the other half onto the front deck. That tree was not much taller than I am when Robyn, my wife, and I moved out here to Mountain Township, Ont., in 1987. Now it's gone.

Our 12-day trial by firelight was not life-threatening, but was surely a reminder of the fragility of our nordic existence, of my addiction to electronic gadgetry, and of the labour required to live like a settler.

By the last week of January, some 300 customers in Ontario and 45 000 in Quebec were still powerless. Doug Thompson, mayor of Osgoode Township, Ont., promised not to lift his state of emergency until power was restored to every last house. By February, the ice storm was, in most newscasts, relegated to the end, an afterthought, as newer news— presidential scandals and weak dollars—took the lead.

One prevailing sentiment echoed across the land: a certainty that things will never be the same. Like many, we vowed we will consume less energy and be less reliant on one source. We will be more sociable with neighbours and strangers. And we will be acutely aware that we are as susceptible as the people of the Saguenay, the Red River, or anywhere else to the destructive power of nature. ■

Investigating the Model

1. An event description often contains a topic sentence that names the subject to be described and establishes the tone (e.g., funny, serious, sad). Locate the topic sentence in the model and assess how well it accomplishes these two goals.

2. A description such as this one can be written for any audience, but the level of language and the choice of detail will change depending on the interests and level of understanding of the intended reader. Who is the audience for this piece of writing? Provide support for your answer.

3. An event description usually follows one of the following organizational patterns: spatial (moving from one location to another), chronological (time), or from an overall impression of the event to specific details that describe it. Identify the organizational pattern of the model.

4. Because it deals with an actual event, an event description must convey information accurately. Read through the model and locate 10 facts that are presented. How does the author make these facts relevant and interesting?

5. An event description is usually written from the narrator's point of view, and includes his or her own subjective impressions of the event. Find 10 examples of language in the model where the writer presents his own opinion or his subjective impression of the ice storm.

6. An event description often contains details that appeal to the five senses—sight, hearing, smell, taste, and touch. Provide five examples from the model (phrases, sentences, or paragraphs) in which the author appeals to the reader's senses. Identify the example you like best and explain why it is your favourite.

7. Unity is created in a piece of writing by ensuring that each paragraph relates back to the introductory paragraph(s). Choose three paragraphs from the body of the model and explain how they are related to the introductory paragraph at the beginning of the piece.

Checkpoint: Event Description

✓ As a class, create a checklist of common features of event descriptions, based on what you have just learned. You can use the checklist to help you create your own event description.

Writer's Workshop

1. Make a list of important events you have witnessed or have been a part of recently (for example, a game, a school assembly, a concert or show, something special that happened on a trip, a ceremony, a special visit, a time you will never forget). Choose one that you would like to describe.

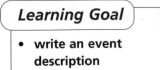

Learning Goal

- **write an event description**

2. List the who, what, where, when, how, and why of the event. You may want to interview others who were there to make sure you have all the information you need. In addition, try to gather some interesting statistics about the event.

3. List details of your experience of the event related to each of the five senses.

4. Look over the notes that you have written, and decide on what overall impression you want to give. Was it scary? exciting? historic? humorous? Write a topic sentence that describes this dominant impression.

5. Decide on a way to organize your information. Remember that it does not have to be chronological.

6. Write a draft of your event description. Make sure each paragraph helps to support the dominant impression in your topic sentence.

7. Conclude by summarizing or drawing a conclusion from your experience. For example, you might explain
   - why this event was worthwhile or important to you and others
   - why you would or would not like to relive the event
   - the significance of the event to you, to the community, or to others

☑ 8. Refer back to the list you created at Checkpoint, and revise and edit your description until you are satisfied with its focus, content, and organization.

Oral Language Extension

In "Struck Powerless" several heroes were identified: the Hydro-Québec linemen, the broadcasters, the neighbours, the soldiers, and the volunteers. For this activity, your class will be divided into five equal groups, one group representing each of these heroes. Your group of heroes is to be interviewed by the media, but you are not sure what questions you will be asked.

1. In preparation for your interview, your group should do the following:
   - Make a list of five questions that you think the media might ask you about your role in the ice storm.
   - Jot down some ideas to answer each of the questions identified.
   - Decide who will answer the first question asked, the second, etc.
   - Rehearse your answers to the questions.

2. Identify one person in your group to interview another group of heroes (your teacher will tell you which group that will be). As a group, develop five questions the designated interviewer will ask. Review your questions to make sure they are well developed (e.g., cannot be answered either "yes" or "no").

3. Carry out the interviews under the direction of your teacher.

DESCRIPTION

Grammar

Parallel structure exists when writers use words, phrases, clauses, or sentences with similar grammatical structures or functions.

Learning Goal

- select and use parallel structures

Linking together words or ideas in a series is a powerful way to create an impression in descriptive writing. Whenever possible, express parallel ideas in a parallel grammatical form.

Dairy farmers, apple growers, and **sugarbush owners** struggled to quantify their losses.

A stalement ensued, with **warm air above** and **cool air below**.

Our 12-day trial by firelight ... was a reminder **of the fragility of our nordic existence, of my addiction to electronic gadgetry**, and **of the labour required to live like a settler**.

1. In groups of four, discuss the parallel structure in the above examples. Be prepared to explain exactly which elements are parallel, and why.

WRITING TIP

One way to make sure similar elements of a sentence are parallel is to write them as a chart on a separate piece of paper. For example

COMMON ELEMENT

Every tree was	snapped	at the crown
	cracked	at major limbs
	bent over	with tips frozen into the shining ground.

2. Each of the following passages contains a mistake in parallel structure. Use a chart like the one above to analyze the common elements and parallel structures of each sentence. Isolate the error, and suggest a way to correct it.

a) The ice storm provoked a range of reactions, created dangerous situations, and heroes were made.

b) The ice storm raged for six days over open farmland, hillsides that were conifer-cloaked, urban grids, and maze-like suburbs.

c) The elderly and infirm were looked after by relief workers, by the military, and an army of volunteers.

d) The heroes were the Hydro workers who risked their lives; the CBC radio broadcasters who fed the airwaves; while neighbours and volunteers looked after those in trouble or need.

3. Choose one passage from the model that contains parallel structure. Make up two more elements using the same structure that could be added to the sentence.

MEDIA LINK

Interview a classmate about an event they have recently witnessed or taken part in (e.g., a game, school assembly, concert, trip, family celebration). Make sure you cover the who, what, when, where, why, and how questions. Using concise paragraphs (two or three sentences only), write up the event for the school newspaper. Use the same information to tape a 30-second radio news item. Practise to make your voice sound confident and expressive. Ambient sound (e.g., background noises from a game; the sound of people cheering) and short interview clips may help.

Mechanics

Number conventions can vary. Informal writing and scientific writing often use numerals for all numbers, while very formal, literary writing may spell out everything from one to infinity.

Learning Goal

- **learn how to present numerical information**

No matter what kind of writing you are doing, it is important to be consistent in your use of numbers. Investigating the numerical style used in the model will give you a sense of how to deal with numbers in your own descriptive writing.

1. For each of the following examples from the model, work with a partner to identify what convention the author followed in presenting numbers (for example, why are some numbers spelled out, while others are written numerically?). Consult a writer's handbook to verify your findings.
   a) ... late on Sunday, January 4 ...
   b) ... loads 30 times their own weight.
   c) ... more than 80 millimetres of ice rain over six days.
   d) The victims: 25 who died in Quebec and Ontario ...
   e) ... estimated damage at $500 million ...
   f) ... 6 a.m. on January 8 ...
   g) A 12-metre green ash ...
   h) ... I moved out here to Mountain Township, Ont., in 1987.
   i) Our 12-day trial by firelight ...
   j) By the last week of January, some 300 customers in Ontario and 45 000 in Quebec were still powerless.

2. Create a Number Style Guide for your classroom. In your guide, include all the conventions you gathered in activity #1. In addition, research and include information on how to present the following numerical information:
   a) percentages
   b) temperatures
   c) numbers that appear as the first word in a sentence
   d) page numbers

e) addresses

f) decimals

g) telephone numbers

h) postal codes

i) a number that comes before a compound modifier that includes another number

For each guideline, include a sentence or example to illustrate it. Publish your guide and keep it in the classroom for reference.

3. Use your class style guide to edit your own event description.

WRITING TIP

Presenting a list of statistics in your description can either bore your reader or capture his or her attention. The key is to find the best way to present the data. Here are some suggestions:

- Make big numbers understandable by comparing them to something more familiar. (Tracts of green ash and cedar, white pine and willow splintered violently under loads 30 times their own weight.)

- Unless accuracy is important, round numbers off rather than giving precise amounts. ("The storm flooded a rink greater than the Great Lakes with *more than 80 millimetres* of ice rain ...")

- Always have a clear reason for including numerical data: it's best to avoid overloading your writing with numbers unless you feel they are the best way to convey your information.

Usage & Style

Use precise nouns and vivid verbs.

When you think of description, the words that probably come to mind are modifiers: adjectives and adverbs. While modifiers can help to enrich a sentence, they are no substitute for well-chosen nouns and verbs. Compare the following examples.

Every tree was badly *broken* in some way.	Every tree, and there are hundreds, was *snapped* at the crown, *cracked* at major limbs, or *bent over* with tips frozen into the shining ground.
Farmers tried hard to quantify their losses.	*Dairy farmers, apple growers, and sugarbush owners struggled* to quantify their losses.

Learning Goal

- use precise and interesting nouns, verbs, and modifiers

While both the left-hand and the right-hand sentences convey the same information, those on the right are more descriptive and vivid. Here are three tips to help you write more vivid descriptions:

- **Use precise nouns** ("dairy farmers," "apple growers," and "sugarbush owners" instead of just "farmers").

- **Choose vivid verbs** ("snapped," "cracked," "bent over" instead of just "broken").

- **Use modifiers** (adjectives and adverbs) **only when you cannot find a single noun or verb that expresses your meaning** ("struggled" instead of "tried hard").

1. From the model, list five verbs, three nouns, and three modifiers that you found particularly effective. Compare your choices with those of a partner, and discuss the reasons for your preferences.

2. Read the following sentences. Then find a way to make each one more interesting by using precise nouns, vivid verbs, or more effective modifiers.
   a) The region was covered in ice.
   b) The storm showed how much we rely on electricity.
   c) Senior citizens were stuck in their houses without heat.
   d) Hydro crews worked long hours to repair the broken lines.
   e) Shelters were full of people.

3. Read over your event description, and look for ways to make your nouns, verbs, and modifiers more effective.

TECHNO-TIP

An excellent way to find nouns that are more specific is to use the thesaurus on your word processing program. Synonyms and antonyms are provided so that you can choose precise words. Be sure to check their meaning in a dictionary if you are unfamiliar with them.

Word Study & Spelling

To create a memorable description, you used images that appeal to more than one sense; similarly, you can use your senses to help you remember how to spell certain words. Here are some ideas.

Note: For more spelling strategies, see Unit 3.

Sounding Strategies

- Sound the word out in your head or out loud. This works fine for words that are spelled exactly the way they sound (e.g., *reminder, humanitarian*).

- Use correct pronunciation. You may spell some words incorrectly because you do not pronounce them correctly (e.g., *extraordinary*, not *extrordinary*, *February* not *Febuary*, *probably* not *probly*).

> ### Learning Goal
> - **use knowledge of spelling strategies to correct spelling errors**

- Exaggerate hidden sounds. Some sounds are difficult to hear when you say the word normally. Exaggerating these sounds can help you to spell it (e.g., *intEresting, exHausted*).

TECHNO-TIP

Computer spell-check programs are useful for catching some spelling errors, but they will not notice errors such as using "it's" instead of "its," or "weigh" instead of "way." Always check spelling yourself, then let the computer do a final check.

- Say longer words one syllable at a time (e.g., *mil-len-ni-um, me-te-or-o-log-i-cal, hy-per-bol-ic-al-ly*).

- Think of another word with the same pattern (e.g., *stealth—wealth, weight—eight*)

Visual Strategies

- Highlight difficult letters (e.g., *fraGility, existEnce, soCiable*)

- Draw the shape of the word.

- Visualize the word. Look closely at the spelling of a word, and then close your eyes. Visualize the word spelled out in your head. Do this a few times; then, write the word on a piece of paper and check the spelling.

WORD ORIGINS

Many words that are considered distinctly Canadian in their use or origin have come to us through the French Canadian settlers in Quebec. For example, a **tuque** is a French Canadian name for a winter hat. **Toboggan** is another distinctly Canadian word that French settlers picked up from Algonkian, and passed on to English. Look up the meaning and origins of each of the following Canadianisms. Which of these words came to us through French Canadian settlers? Can you name some other distinctly Canadian words or phrases?

poutine   muskeg   tourtiere   allophone   muskie   chinook

Tactile Strategies

- Trust your instincts: if a spelling does not "feel" right, it probably isn't. Try writing the word several ways, or check it in a dictionary.

1. Using your notes and previous edited assignments, write a list of 10 words that often cause you spelling problems. Beside each word, write a strategy that could help you to remember its spelling.

2. On pages 214–216 of this text is a list of frequently misspelled words in student and adult writing. Choose five words from the list and identify why each word may cause difficulty. Create a learning aid for each word to help you remember the correct spelling: a mnemonic rhyme or sentence; a visual reminder.

Looking Back

Before handing in your final edited draft, have a classmate check your event description, paying particular attention to the following:

 Are parallel structures used correctly and effectively?

 Is numerical information written correctly and consistently?

 Has the writer used precise nouns, vivid verbs, and interesting modifiers?

 Are all words spelled correctly?

Reflect and Build on Your Learning

Reflecting on Descriptive Writing Forms

1. Review the Learning Goals on page 65. Which goals do you think you have achieved most successfully? Which goals do you think will require you to do more work? Why?

2. This section covered three forms of description. What other forms of descriptive writing do you know? (You may wish to review the features of description on page 64.) Choose one of them and describe its features to a partner, explaining *why* and *when* you would use it. Does your partner agree with your explanation? Would you change anything you've said because of his or her feedback? In what way?

Looking Over Descriptive Writing Forms

1. Working with a small group, discuss what you know about poetry, profiles, and event descriptions. To guide your discussion, create a chart that includes these three forms, as well as the additional form you chose for activity #2 above. Develop five criteria for comparing the forms. One criterion might be use of sensory details. Complete the chart to compare the four forms. Compare your chart with those of other groups. How would you modify your chart based on what they have included in theirs?

CRITERIA	POETRY	PROFILE	EVENT DESCRIPTION	OTHER
Sensory details				

Using the Descriptive Writing Forms

1. For a class collection of poetry, write a descriptive poem of a place in your community that you know well, using as a guide the class checklist of features for this form. Revise your draft to make sure that it is vivid and unified in the images and mood it is trying to convey. Edit and proofread your poem carefully, especially for the checklist of items on page 81. If possible, you may want to videotape images of the place to accompany a class presentation of the poem.

2. Write a profile of a historical figure who interests you, using as a guide the class checklist of features for this form. Have a classmate read a draft of your profile, also using the class checklist as a guide. Revise your profile as needed, and have your classmate edit and proofread it carefully, especially for the checklist of items on page 95. If you prefer, present the information on the historical figure in the form of an imagined interview. In this case, make sure to prepare five or six key questions to help your "interviewee" focus on important details about his or her life and career.

3. Working with a partner, choose an event description from a large-circulation newspaper or magazine that you would like to rewrite for the school newspaper. Identify the dominant organizational pattern (e.g., spatial) used in the original description, and decide on two alternative patterns for organizing the description. You and your partner should each choose one of the alternative patterns and rewrite the description to fit the pattern chosen. Rearrange, add, and delete details as needed. Read each other's drafts, and evaluate each for the relevance, accuracy, and completeness of the information provided. Keep in mind the original description, the organizational pattern used, and the class checklist of features for event descriptions. Revise your draft based on your partner's feedback. Have your partner edit and proofread your description carefully, especially for the checklist of items on page 109.

4. Write a short essay evaluating the relevance, accuracy, and completeness of the information provided in the newspaper description of an event that you witnessed. Use as a guide the class checklist of features for event descriptions. Revise drafts of your essay to ensure that each of your paragraphs has a clear topic sentence, sufficient supporting details, and appropriate connecting words. Have a classmate carefully edit and proofread your essay.

BUILD ON YOUR LEARNING

Exposition

Expository writing is writing at work. It deals in facts, not fancy, and it is focused on what the reader needs to know. But although it is functional, there's quite an art to good expository writing. If you've ever been frustrated by a confusing instruction manual or an unreadable explanation, you know already that exposition demands more than simply answering who, what, when, where, why, and how. Careful choice of wording and content and a logical organization designed to meet the needs of the reader are crucial as well.

This section contains three forms of expository writing: explanation, précis, and research report. Although these forms are very different from one another, each presents factual information in a format that is useful and understandable to the reader.

Features of Exposition

- Exposition involves presenting facts to a specific audience.
- Expository writing is arranged to make information as accessible and understandable to the reader as possible.
- Expository writers often define unfamiliar or technical terms by comparing them with something more familiar to the reader.
- The writer's personal opinions and value judgments are usually not part of expository writing.

Learning Goals

- use print and electronic sources to gather information and explore ideas for your written work

- identify and use informational forms appropriately in writing an explanation, a précis, and a research report

- use organizational techniques to present ideas and supporting details

- revise your written work independently and collaboratively

- edit and proofread to produce final drafts using correct grammar, spelling, and punctuation

- use knowledge of vocabulary and language conventions; for example, use transitive and intransitive verbs correctly

- develop listening, speaking, and media literacy skills

- read a variety of nonfiction, such as explanation, précis, and research report

- identify and understand the elements and style of a variety of nonfiction

Unit 7 Explanation

What is an explanation?

An explanation often tells how or why something happens. It describes a cause-and-effect relationship in language the intended audience can understand. Explanations are especially useful in the sciences, but they are also used in business and elsewhere. In the following piece, author Ira Flatow explains in simple language how a rainbow is formed.

Learning Goals

- write an explanation
- use direct and indirect objects, transitive and intransitive verbs, and subject complements
- learn proper punctuation for definitions
- explain the use of active and passive voice in explanations
- recognize Greek and Latin word roots

Why Must Rainbows Be Curved?

BY IRA FLATOW

... ONCE WHILE DRIVING THROUGH THE FOREST, I EMERGED
from the darkness of the towering trees to stumble upon the breathtaking
sight of a rainbow. Actually, two rainbows, one inside the other. While I was
marvelling at my luck, my travelling companion,
knowing my penchant for science trivia, asked me
why rainbows are curved. Why can't they be
endless multicoloured bands unfolding like
streamers across the sky?... The answer, of course,
involves understanding what rainbows are and
how they are formed.

The explanation begins with rain. Rainbows
come out only in the rain or right after it rains
because raindrops are responsible for producing
the colours. As you know, sunlight is composed of
all the colours of the rainbow. Isaac Newton
pointed out that sunlight streaming through a
prism will be broken up into a spectrum of
colours ranging from red to violet. A drop of
water will have the same effect. As shown in

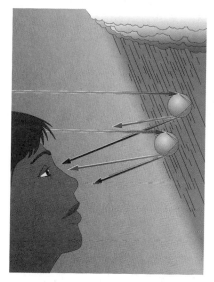

Illustration 1

Illustration 1, a rainbow's development begins when sunlight enters the
front of a raindrop, gets bent, and is separated into its constituent colours.
The colours bounce off the back of the drop and are bent again, exiting
through the front.

So out of white light comes colour. Notice that the light enters the drop
in a straight line but leaves the drop having been bent (refracted) and
bounced by the water. The amount of bending varies from colour to colour.
So as they come out, the red and blue rays—and all the colours in
between—exit at different angles and go in different directions. The angle
of deflection for each colour also varies, from about 40 degrees for blue to
about 42 degrees for red, with gradations of other colours in between. The
difference in the angle of deflection explains why the colours are spread out
into a multicoloured band, red at the top and blue near the bottom.

It would appear that if all it takes to turn sunlight into colours is a collection of raindrops, we should be seeing rainbows quite often—during every rainstorm and shower, in fact. But we don't. Why? It's true that rainbows are being created, but to see them, you and the sun must be in the right position with respect to one another. The sun must be at just the right height in the sky so that the angle formed by the sun, the raindrop, and you is just right. This angle is the same angle of deflection shown in the illustration, about 42 degrees. For the rainbow to be seen, the sun must be positioned in the sky so that the light entering the drops (sunlight) and the colours meeting your eyes form this critical angle....

Illustration 2

Notice that the sun must be behind you (Illustration 2) in order for you to see the rainbow, and the light must shine on distant air laden with storm raindrops; it's like being in a movie theatre with the sun acting as film projector and the dark storm clouds serving as the screen....

Finally, about that question of why rainbows are bowed. Try this thought experiment. Give yourself a paintbrush and canvas (or paper and pencil) and the job of painting a band in the sky, knowing that (1) your hand, representing a person viewing the band, has to remain fixed in position and (2) the band has to be maintained at about a 42-degree angle wherever you looked. How would you draw it? The only way would be to sweep your hand back and forth across the paper without moving your fingers or lifting your hand.

Isn't it intuitively obvious that the only way to maintain the angle is to create an arc? Only in an arc, or in a complete circle, are all the raindrops at the same angle to the sun. Any drops above or below the band would violate the 42-degree angle.

As you walked, the rainbow would "walk" with you, maintaining the same angle. Furthermore, if the ground could somehow be taken away, the rainbow would continue to arc and come around to form a full circle. One way to remove the ground is to get high enough in the air. Rainbow "circles" are quite common sights to occupants of an airplane flying by sunlit clouds, or perhaps to someone looking over the edge of a high, steep mountain. ■

Investigating the Model

1. An explanation often begins with a question or statement and then provides the answer or supplies details to back up the assertion. What question or statement is presented in the model? What other purposes does the opening paragraph serve?

2. An explanation usually proceeds step by step, or moves from cause to effect (or effect to cause). Identify an example of each of these patterns in the model.

3. Explanations are often supported by visual aids, such as diagrams or illustrations. How effective did you find the illustrations that accompany the model? What other aspects of the explanation do you think could or should have been illustrated?

4. Writers of explanations often use analogies (comparing an unfamiliar subject with something more familiar) to assist a nonspecialist reader to understand the phenomenon. Identify two examples of analogies in the model, and comment on their effectiveness.

5. The language, amount of detail, and use of technical terms in an explanation depend on the expertise of the audience for whom it is written. Who is the audience for this piece of writing? Provide support for your answer.

Checkpoint: Explanation

☑ As a class, create a checklist of common features of an explanation, based on what you have just learned. The checklist can be used to help you write your own explanation.

Writer's Workshop

1. For this writing assignment, your audience will be students in younger grades, aged 7 to 10. Working in groups of four, brainstorm a list of possible topics for an explanation aimed at this age group.

IDEA FILE

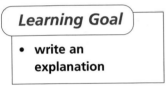

To help you get started, think of the explanations that you have studied in various subjects in school over the past few years, including English; or develop some out-of-the-ordinary topics such as: How are potato chips made? or Why do black jeans go grey when you wash them?

2. Choose one of the explanations that you would like to describe. Make sure that the subject is narrow enough to allow you to explain it in no more than three pages.

Learning Goal

• **write an explanation**

3. Gather facts and details about your topic that will be interesting and understandable to your audience. Some possible sources for your facts are textbooks, popular science books, encyclopedias, Web sites, science centres, or people (interviews).

4. Decide whether you will begin with the cause or the effect, and create an idea web or a chart to help you arrange the details you have in a logical order. Also, consider what terms or concepts you will need to explain for the reader.

5. Write a draft of your explanation. Make sure you have provided enough detail for your readers to understand clearly, but not so much that they get confused (remember their age). Use transition words like *next, then,* or *so* to help them follow the explanation.

   Note: For more about transition words, see Unit 9, or the list of transitions on page 206.

6. If you haven't already done so, add an introductory and concluding sentence or paragraph to your explanation.

7. Revise your work using the list you developed in Checkpoint. If possible, try your explanation out on students in the age range you were writing for, and make changes based on their reaction.

Oral Language Extension

Prepare a demonstration of a process, aimed at the same audience as your written explanation. If applicable, base your demonstration on the process you described. Keep your presentation to under five minutes, and review the Speaking Skills section, on page 204, as you prepare your presentation. Before you perform, consider the following questions:

- What level of vocabulary will you need to use to communicate with your audience?

- What props or visual aids might be helpful? (Consider using demonstrations, overheads, charts, or illustrations.)

- How can you involve your audience in the presentation? (What questions could you ask them? If you are performing a demonstration, could you use a student as a helper?)

If possible, try out your presentation in front of an audience of younger students, and ask them for feedback; or, give the demonstration to a group of your peers, and ask them if they thought your level of language and method of presentation were suitable for a younger audience.

Grammar

An important part of any explanation is terminology. Knowing the correct words to use gives you a more in-depth knowledge of the thing or process being described. This is also true for grammar. Here are some grammar terms you may not be familiar with.

A **direct object** is a noun, noun phrase, or pronoun that receives the action of an action verb, and answers the questions *what*, or *whom*.

A collection of raindrops **can turn** *sunlight* into colours.
      verb   *direct object*

An **indirect object** is a noun or pronoun that tells *to whom* or *for whom* something is done or given.

Give   <u>yourself</u> *a paintbrush and canvas.*
verb <u>indirect object</u>   *direct object*

Learning Goal

- use direct and indirect objects, transitive and intransitive verbs, and subject complements

1. Identify any direct and indirect objects in the following sentences.
   a) Try an experiment.
   b) My travelling companion asked me a question.
   c) I gave my companion an explanation.
   d) The light enters the drop in a straight line.
   e) Mother Nature provides the raindrop with sunlight.
   f) We noticed them in the distance.

2. Write two sentences of your own that contain a direct and an indirect object.

A verb that needs a direct object to complete its meaning is called a **transitive verb**; a verb that does not need a direct object is called an **intransitive verb**.

Note that many verbs can be transitive or intransitive depending on the context.

Transitive: The prism **bends** *the light.*

Intransitive: The arc **bends** in a circle.

3. Identify the verbs in the following sentences and indicate whether they are transitive or intransitive.
   a) The angle of deflection for each colour varies.
   b) The colours meet your eyes at a 42-degree angle.
   c) Rainbows emerge only during or right after a rainstorm.
   d) The drops of water deflect the sunlight.

4. Write four sentences of your own, two containing a transitive verb, and two containing an intransitive verb.

In addition to transitive and intransitive verbs, there are linking verbs (*is, seems, appears, feels, smells, looks, sounds, tastes,* etc.). Linking verbs never take a direct object; instead, they may be followed by a subject complement.

A **subject complement** is a noun or adjective that renames or describes the subject. It is connected to the subject by a **linking verb**.

subject	linking verb	subject complement
The rainbow	appears	curved.

The sky	is	blue.
The air	smells	fresh.

Some verbs can act as either a linking verb or an action verb.

Linking: Your explanation **sounded** good.

Action: I **sounded** the alarm.

WRITING TIP

An easy way to tell if a verb is a linking verb is to try replacing it with a form of the verb "be." If the meaning of the sentence is unchanged, the verb is a linking verb.

5. Identify the subject complement in each of the following sentences, and indicate whether it describes the subject or renames the subject.
   a) The rainbow was captivating.
   b) A prism is a solid glass object.
   c) The raindrops are little prisms.
   d) Rainbow "circles" are quite common.
   e) The rainbow seems faded.

6. In groups of five, prepare a brief oral explanation of the grammar concepts covered in this unit. Try to find an innovative way to explain the terms (e.g., a rap tune, a demonstration, a skit). Present your explanation to the class.

7. Examine your explanation. Find one example of each of the following: direct object, indirect object, subject complement, transitive verb, intransitive verb.

MEDIA LINK

Analytical videos are used by athletes, actors, musicians, and speakers to help them analyze details of their performance. Arrange to tape an analytical video at school. Possible topics might be: specific game skills, gymnastic movements, debating techniques, drama rehearsals, scientific experiments. Slow-motion, freeze-frame, and fast-motion playback can reveal details and patterns of movement that might be difficult to see at normal speeds. How would you use these special effects in your video?

Mechanics

As you write your explanation, you may have to define some unfamiliar terms for your readers. You could simply add a sentence explaining what the term means, or you can find ways to work the information into your writing without breaking the flow of your explanation, using parentheses, dashes, or a colon.

Parentheses: Notice that the light enters the drop in a straight line but leaves the drop having been bent (refracted) and bounced by the water.

Dashes: Notice that the light enters the drop in a straight line but leaves the drop having been bent—refracted—and bounced by the water.

Colon: Notice that the light enters the drop in a straight line but leaves the drop having been bent by the water: this is known as refraction.

1. With a partner, discuss the difference in emphasis in these three ways of defining the term *refraction*. Which method would you use if you wanted to emphasize the definition more? Which method would you use if you wanted to de-emphasize the term?

2. Rewrite each of the following sentences in one of the three ways shown above, adding a simple definition of the word in italics. (Use a dictionary if you are unsure what the term means.) Try using a different method for each of the three sentences. Can you think of any other ways to include the definitions, other than those that have been discussed?
   a) You can break sunlight into a rainbow by passing it through a *prism*.
   b) The angle of *deflection* varies for each colour.
   c) Isaac Newton pointed out that sunlight streaming through a prism will be broken up into a *spectrum* of colours ranging from red to violet.

3. Look for terms that may need to be explained in your explanation. Consider using one of the methods above to insert information, if necessary.

Usage & Style

Use the **passive voice** when the doer of the action is unimportant or unknown. In all other cases, use the **active voice**.

In the active voice, the subject *performs* the action. In the passive voice, the subject *receives* the action. When the verb is in the passive voice, the positions of the direct object and the subject are reversed. Only transitive verbs can be written in the passive voice.

> **Learning Goal**
>
> - explain the use of active and passive voice in explanations

Isaac Newton first **noticed** the refraction of sunlight.

The refraction of sunlight **was noticed** first by Isaac Newton.

Although the active voice is usually a better choice, the passive voice is useful in cause-and-effect explanations because it can help to emphasize the cause (what happens) as opposed to the effect (who does it). Notice the difference in emphasis in the following sentences:

Active: The raindrop bends the light that travels through it. (Focus is on what the raindrop does.)

Passive: The light is bent as it travels through the raindrop. (Focus is on what happens to the light.)

1. Working in groups of four, reread the model and identify two sentences that are written in the passive voice. Rewrite them in the active voice, and decide which version is more appropriate in the context, and why.

2. **a)** With a partner, find an example of an explanation that uses passive voice in a science textbook or a science encyclopedia. Try rewriting the explanation using only the active voice. Share your results with another group, and discuss any difficulties you encountered. Which version do you think is clearer?

   b) Look through several instruction manuals that give step-by-step instructions on how to perform a task. Do these manuals use mainly active or passive voice? With a partner, discuss why you think this is the case.

3. Look through your explanation for examples of sentences written in the passive voice. Decide whether you are justified in using the passive voice, and change any sentences that you think should be active.

TECHNO-TIP

Some software programs identify the passive voice in sentences in order to determine whether or not the writer wishes to change to the active voice. If such a program exists on your computer at school or at home, try it.

Word Study & Spelling

Learning Goal

- **recognize Greek and Latin word roots**

Although the English language began to develop in what is now Great Britain, it evolved from a number of different sources, among them Celtic languages, German dialects, Latin, and Norman French, which contained many Greek and Latin words.

1. Look up each of the following words from the model in an etymological dictionary. Identify the Latin root word it contains. Then find at least one other English word that contains the same root.
   a) producing
   b) spectrum
   c) refracted
   d) deflection
   e) directions
   f) degree
   g) gradations
   h) difference
   i) position

2. Many of the terms we use to discuss scientific disciplines come from Greek root words. Think of as many words as you can that contain the following Greek roots.
   a) bios (life)
   b) micro (small)

c) macro (large)
d) kilo (thousand)
e) geo (earth)
f) eco (house, environment)
g) zoo (animal)
h) bi (two)
i) logy (study of)
j) sophy (love of)
k) graph (to write)

WORD ORIGINS

Traditionally, scientific terms have been based on Latin and Greek words. In recent times, however, with the explosion of scientific discoveries in areas such as physics, scientists have become a bit more adventuresome in their choice of names. Read books about language and word origins to find some interesting word origins for science- or technology-related terms. Choose one and explain its meaning and origin to the class. Here are some examples to get you started.

googol   niacin   quasar   bit/byte   boot up (a computer)

Looking Back

Before handing in your final draft, have a classmate check your explanation, paying particular attention to the following:

 Have any words that may cause difficulty to the audience been explained adequately?

 Are definitions worked into the text using appropriate punctuation?

 Have the passive voice and the active voice been used appropriately and effectively?

 Are all words spelled correctly?

Unit **8** Précis

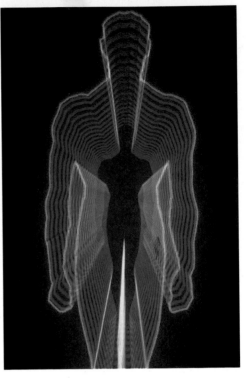

What is a précis?

A précis (pronounced PRAY-see) is a summary that contains the main ideas of a written passage. In school, you may write a précis to summarize your research findings. Business reports often begin with a kind of précis called an abstract that summarizes the contents of the report. The model that follows is a précis of an article about the future of computer technology. The original article follows the précis.

Learning Goals

- **write a précis**
- **recognize and correct run-on sentences and comma splices**
- **punctuate essential and nonessential clauses correctly**
- **identify and explain examples of jargon**
- **use a dictionary and thesaurus for finding word replacements**

When Machines Think (Précis)

IN THE 21ST CENTURY, MACHINES WILL BE MORE INTELLIGENT than their creators. By 2019, a $1000 computer will match the processing power of the human brain, and by 2029, it will be equivalent to 1000 human brains.

Computers can easily share their knowledge with billions of other computers. By the time computers become as intelligent as humans, they will become masters of all human and machine-acquired knowledge.

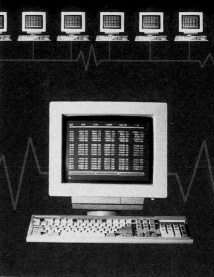

There will not be a clear distinction between human and machine as we go through the 21st century. We will be putting computers—neural implants—into our brains. We already have neural implants to treat Parkinson's disease and other conditions. More are under development.

Virtual reality will become as realistic, detailed, and subtle as real reality.

Computers, which are built from integrated circuits, are doubling in power every two years. By 2030, it will take a village of human brains to match a $1000 computer; by around 2055, a $1000 computer will equal the processing power of all human brains.

Brain-scanning technologies are rapidly increasing their ability to solve problems. The next generation will enable us to peer inside the synapses and record the neurotransmitter strengths. This development will enable us to copy a brain's design, including the contents of its memory.

Consciousness will be a critical issue. At what point will a computer become conscious, feel pain and discomfort, and have its own free will?

Before the next century is over, there will be few differences between human brains and computers. This development will be as important as the evolution of human intelligence thousands of years ago. (268 words) ∎

When Machines Think

BY RAY KURZWEIL

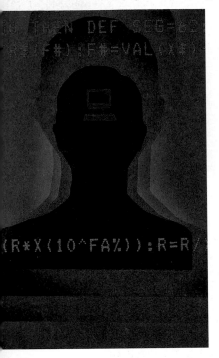

A THRESHOLD EVENT WILL TAKE PLACE EARLY IN THE 21ST century: the emergence of machines more intelligent than their creators. By 2019, a $1000 computer will match the processing power of the human brain—about 20-million-billion calculations per second. Organizing these resources—the "software" of intelligence—will take us to 2029, by which time your average personal computer will be equivalent to 1000 human brains.

Once a computer achieves a level of intelligence comparable to human intelligence, it will necessarily soar past it. For one thing, computers can easily share their knowledge. If I learn French, or read *War and Peace*, I can't readily download that learning to you. You have to acquire that scholarship the same painstaking way that I did. But if one computer learns a skill or gains an insight, it can immediately share that wisdom with billions of other computers. So every computer can be a master of all human and machine-acquired knowledge.

Keep in mind that this is not an alien invasion of intelligent machines. It is emerging from within our civilization. There will not be a clear distinction between human and machine as we go through the 21st century.

First of all, we will be putting computers—neural implants—directly into our brains. We have already started down this path. We have neural implants to counteract Parkinson's disease and tremors from multiple sclerosis. We have cochlear implants that restore hearing to deaf individuals. Under development is a retina implant that will perform a similar function for blind people, basically replacing the visual processing circuits of the brain. Recently, scientists from Emory University in Atlanta placed a chip in the brain of a paralyzed stroke victim, who can now begin to communicate and control his environment directly from his brain.

In the 2020s, neural implants will not be just for people with disabilities. There will be ubiquitous use of neural implants to improve our sensory experiences, perception, memory, and logical thinking. These implants will also plug us in directly to the World Wide Web. This technology will enable us to have virtual reality experiences with other people—or simulated people—without requiring any equipment not already in our heads.

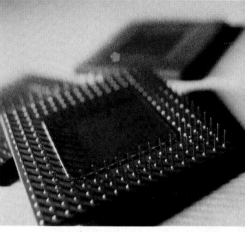

And virtual reality will not be the crude experience that you may have experienced today in arcade games. Virtual reality will be as realistic, detailed, and subtle as real reality. So instead of just phoning a friend, you can meet in a virtual French café in Paris, or stroll down a virtual Champs Elysées, and it will seem very real.

The next 20 years will see far more change than the previous hundred. One very important trend is referred to as "Moore's Law." Gordon Moore, one of the inventors of integrated circuits, and then chairman of Intel, noted in the mid-1970s that we could squeeze twice as many transistors on an integrated circuit every 24 months. The implication is that computers, which are built from integrated circuits, are doubling in power every two years. Lately, the rate has been even faster. So where will this take us? By 2030, it will take a village of human brains to match a $1000 personal computer. By 2055, a thousand dollars of computing will equal the processing power of all human brains on Earth. OK, I may be off a year or two.

There are a number of compelling scenarios to capture higher levels of intelligence in our computers, and ultimately human levels and beyond. Let me describe one particularly critical scenario. There is no reason why we cannot reverse engineer the human brain, and essentially copy its design. Brain-scanning technologies are increasing their resolution with each new generation. The next generation will enable us to resolve the connections between neurons. Ultimately, we will be able to peer inside the synapses and record the neurotransmitter strengths. Once we reach this stage, we could copy someone's brain to map the locations, interconnections, and contents of all the somas, axons, dendrites, presynaptic vesicles, and other neural components. Its entire organization could then be recreated on a neural computer of sufficient capacity, including the contents of its memory.

Consciousness in our 21st-century machines will be a critically important issue. But it is not easily resolved, or even readily understood. We don't worry, at least not yet, about causing pain and suffering to our computer programs. But at what point do we consider an entity, a process, to be conscious, to feel pain and discomfort, to have its own intentionality, its own free will?

Before the next century is over, Earth's technology-creating species will merge with its computational technology. After all, what is the difference between a human brain enhanced a trillionfold by neural implants, and a computer whose design is based on high-resolution scans of the human brain, extended a trillionfold? And this development will be no less important than the evolution, thousands of centuries ago, of human intelligence itself. (828 words) ■

Investigating the Model

1. A précis should be about one-third the length of the original passage. What types of information have been cut from the original to reduce the model to one-third of its length?

2. A précis presents only main ideas and omits nonessential details. Find five examples of details from the original article that have been omitted in the précis. Find two details that have been included in the précis. Why do you think these were included?

3. A précis eliminates unimportant ideas, repetition, multiple examples, illustrations of ideas, and figurative language. Working with a partner, compare the précis with the original article. Find specific examples of at least three of these types of omissions.

4. You may use phrases or even whole sentences directly from the original document in a précis. However, ideas that can be condensed or reworded more efficiently should be revised. Find four examples where the model précis rewords an original idea more efficiently.

5. A précis usually copies the same level of formality and tone of the original. Describe the tone and level of formality of the original article, and evaluate how well the author of the précis has managed to imitate them.

Checkpoint: Précis

☑ As a class, create a checklist of common features of a précis based on what you have learned. You can use the checklist to help you write your own précis.

Writer's Workshop

1. Either your teacher will assign you an article to précis, or you will be allowed to choose one of your own. If you choose your own, make sure that it is no more than two pages in length, and that you can understand all the ideas in it. Assume that your intended reader knows very little about your topic.

> **Learning Goal**
> * **write a précis**

2. Read the article once quickly. As you are reading, ask yourself the following questions:
   * To whom is the author speaking?
   * Generally, what is the author saying in this article?
   * What are the main ideas the author is presenting?

3. Read the article again, more slowly. Using a pencil, underline the main point in the introduction and the conclusion. Underline headings and subheadings, and the topic sentence of each paragraph, if they exist. If they don't, write a title, phrase, or short sentence beside each paragraph that captures its main point.

4. Read each paragraph and eliminate the following:
   * unimportant ideas
   * ideas or words that are repeated
   * most examples or illustrations
   * figurative language (if necessary, replace similes and metaphors with a straightforward way of saying the same thing)

5. Using the ideas you have left, write a rough draft of your précis. As you write, it may be necessary for you to reword some ideas.

6. Reread your rough draft. Add to it any transition words needed to make your writing flow more smoothly. Change the sentence structure of any sentences that seem awkward or unclear.

7. Before writing a final draft, revise your précis further using the checklist you developed in Checkpoint.

Oral Language Extension

Taking notes from a live speaker is another type of summary. But unlike a written précis of a book or magazine, with spoken material you may only hear the message once. Therefore, it requires careful listening and notetaking.

Read the article that you based your written précis on out loud to a partner. Read slowly and clearly, placing emphasis on transitions, and pausing to stress important ideas. You may add your own comments to clarify meaning or expand on a certain point. The listening partner should take careful notes, and ask questions when he or she needs clarification.

Afterward, your partner should use his or her notes to give you an oral summary of the article. Point out any crucial information that was missed, and discuss how your partner's oral summary compares with your written summary.

Switch places, and let your partner read to you while you take notes and summarize his or her article.

Grammar

A **run-on sentence** is two or more sentences written as one. A **comma splice** is a type of run-on sentence in which two sentences are separated only by a comma.

Learning Goal

- recognize and correct run-on sentences and comma splices

It's easy to create run-on sentences or comma splices accidentally when you are trying to pack a lot of ideas in a small space, as in a précis.

1. Examine the following pairs of sentences. For each pair, identify how the run-on sentence or comma splice was corrected.

Wrong: The future holds all sorts of possibilities, for example, we may be able to increase our brain power a thousand-fold using neural implants.

Right: The future holds all sorts of possibilities. For example, we may be able to increase our brain power a thousand-fold using neural implants.

Wrong: The article contains some interesting predictions however I'm not sure I agree with all of them.

Right: The article contains some interesting predictions. However, I'm not sure I agree with all of them.

WRITING TIP

Words like *however, nevertheless, in addition*, and *as well* cannot be used to join two clauses into a single sentence. You must begin a new sentence or separate the clauses with a semicolon when you see one of these expressions.

Wrong: Computers can download information to one another this ability allows them to share their knowledge quickly.

Right: Computers can download information to one another, and this ability allows them to share their knowledge quickly.

Wrong: This is not an alien invasion, it will come from within our civilization.

Right: This is not an alien invasion; it will come from within our civilization.

Wrong: Computers in the future will be very intelligent they will be able to solve many major problems.

Right: Since computers in the future will be intelligent, they will be able to solve many major problems.

2. Choose a method from activity #1 and rewrite the following run-on sentences correctly. Explain why you chose that method.
   a) Neural implants will not be just for people with disabilities they will also be used to improve our sensory experiences.
   b) One computer learns a skill, it can immediately share that skill with other computers.

c) Virtual reality will no longer be a crude experience it will be realistic, detailed, and subtle.

d) The future will be great, we have a lot to look forward to.

e) Computers don't have feelings now one day they might.

3. Read over your précis to ensure that you have not included any run-on sentences, including comma splices.

Note: For more on faulty sentence structure, see Unit 12.

MEDIA LINK

In groups, brainstorm a list of science fiction movies that you have seen, and briefly summarize the plot of each film. Use your summaries to create a list of character types, recurring themes, and plot conventions used in science fiction movies (for example, the character who sells out his or her friends; the android). Based on your analysis, create a plot summary of a movie that spoofs (makes fun of by imitating) sci-fi films in general.

Mechanics

As you combine ideas and sentences to reduce the number of words in your précis, you will need to recognize the difference between essential and nonessential information.

> Use **commas** to separate **nonessential clauses** or **phrases** from the rest of the sentence. Never use commas to separate **essential clauses** or **phrases** from the rest of the sentence.

Note: For more on comma use, see Unit 1.

Learning Goal

• punctuate essential and nonessential clauses correctly

A clause is essential if removing it changes the meaning of the sentence. Nonessential clauses give additional information, but the sentence can stand alone without them. Notice how the punctuation of the sentences on the following page changes their meaning.

Essential clause: Computers *that are built from integrated circuits* are doubling in power every two years. (This implies that there are other kinds of computers that are not doubling in power.)

Nonessential clause: Computers, *which are built from integrated circuits*, are doubling in power every two years. (This implies that all computers are built from integrated circuits.)

Some people differentiate essential from nonessential clauses by using *that* for the former and *which* for the latter. However, you will often see essential clauses beginning with *which*.

WRITING TIP

When writing a précis, look for nonessential clauses that can be cut, and use essential and nonessential clauses to combine two or more sentences into one.

1. Rewrite each of the following sentences, inserting the information in parenthesis as an essential (*that*) or nonessential (*which*) clause. Remember to punctuate correctly.
   a) The human brain (has 100 trillion neural connections) is a very complex organism.
   b) Computer consciousness (not an issue yet) will become critically important in the future.
   c) The scanners (we use in medicine today) will be far surpassed by the new generation of scanners.
   d) Should computers (are capable of feeling pain and pleasure) be treated as living things?

2. Explain the difference in meaning in each of the following pairs of sentences.
   a) The future, which Kurzweil forsees, is full of amazing technological advances.
      The future that Kurzweil forsees is full of amazing technological advances.

b) Computers that are modelled on the human brain will soon want the same rights and privileges as people.

Computers, which are modelled on the human brain, will soon want the same rights and privileges as people.

c) Books that a human being would have read from cover to cover can be downloaded from one computer to another in seconds.

Books, which a human being would have to read from cover to cover, can be downloaded from one computer to another in seconds.

d) The quality of virtual reality that we are familiar with today will be vastly improved.

The quality of virtual reality, which we are familiar with today, will look crude when compared to future VR technology.

3. Look through your précis to locate all the *which* and *that* clauses (or write at least two that you could have used). Determine whether each clause is essential or nonessential, and make any necessary changes in punctuation.

Usage & Style

Jargon is the specialized language (often technical terms) used by particular groups of people or professions.

Learning Goal

- identify and explain examples of jargon

Jargon is perfectly acceptable if the document is aimed at a group that understands and uses certain words among themselves. For example, a document aimed at a group of computer experts would not have to explain terms such as "peripheral" or "binary code." To readers who had never used a computer, these terms would look like jargon.

1. Find three examples of jargon in the model précis.

2. Give two examples of jargon you have used this year in each of the following subject areas: science, geography, physical education, mathematics, English.

While jargon can sometimes be useful, writing that is wordy, roundabout, and hard to understand should be simplified. We call this kind of writing

gobbledygook. Unlike jargon, gobbledygook is not easily understood by anyone. People sometimes try to make their writing sound more technical or scientific by adding words and using expressions that are unnecessarily complicated. When you run into writing like this, simplify it.

> **Unclear:**   The actual living through or participating in events such as the invention of human-like computers is likely in the long run to provide incomparable stress.

> **Clear:**   Living in the age of human-like computers will be stressful.

1. Rewrite the sentences below to eliminate wordiness and improve clarity.
   a) In the case of our reaction to this new, improved technology, it is felt by scientists that we will learn to change our thinking in a way that will result in general acceptance.
   b) This millennium we will invent some grand, interesting computers that will not only enable us to reduce our work, but also to do it more easily than we did it before.
   c) One approach to designing intelligent computers will be to copy the human brain, so these machines will seem very human and will begin to act like humans in their behaviour.

Word Study & Spelling

When you are writing a précis, it's a good idea to have a dictionary and a thesaurus close at hand. Use the dictionary to look up the meanings of unfamiliar words in the original. Use the thesaurus to find more precise replacements for words or phrases.

> **Learning Goal**
> - use a dictionary and thesaurus for finding word replacements

1. Before you can use the thesaurus to replace a phrase, you need to identify a key word or idea in the phrase. If possible, that word should be the same part of speech as the word you are searching for. For example, if you want to replace a phrase that is acting as an adjective, then your key word should, if possible, be an adjective. For each of the following phrases or clauses, work with a partner to suggest what word you would use to look up a replacement in a thesaurus.
   a) way of doing something
   b) what is indicated by this
   c) so important that all else depends on it

d) story that shows how things might unfold

e) increasing in speed

> ### WRITING TIP
>
>
>
> Note that the words suggested under a particular heading in the thesaurus may have very different meanings. Don't use a word from the thesaurus that you are not familiar with without looking it up first in a dictionary.

2. Use a thesaurus and your dictionary to find words to replace the underlined phrases in the passage below. Count the words to see how many you saved.

It is hard to <u>make guesses about what will happen next</u>. (11 words)

It is hard to predict the future. (7 words)

a) We can already make a computer that <u>is somewhat like</u> a human brain. (13 words)

b) Once computers can think like humans, they will soon be quicker than we are at <u>gathering together a large amount of</u> information. (22 words)

c) Who is to say that we won't have to <u>give up control of</u> the planet to computers one day? (19 words)

d) The <u>coming together of</u> people and machines is <u>something that is bound to occur</u>. (14 words)

3. With a partner, make a list of other information that is available in a dictionary. Make a poster introducing students from a younger grade to the features of a dictionary. Be sure to include the following features or uses of a dictionary:

- guide words
- pronunciation key
- primary and secondary stress
- word meanings
- parts of speech
- example sentences
- homophones
- homographs
- inflected forms
- etymology
- idioms
- fistnotes
- entry words

WORD ORIGINS

The word **précis** comes from the Latin word *caedere* meaning "to cut." Therefore, a précis is a cut-down version of a longer piece of writing. The following words all come from the same root word. Explain how the meaning of the Latin word *caedere* relates to the meaning of each word as we use it today.

scissors   precise   incisor   decision

Looking Back

Before handing in your final edited draft, have a classmate check your précis, paying particular attention to the following:

 Is the writing free of run-on sentences and comma splices?

✓ Are *which* and *that* clauses punctuated correctly?

✓ Is the tone and language used similar to that of the original?

✓ Could any words or phrases be replaced with more precise words?

Unit 9

Research Report

What is a research report?

Research reports present information from outside sources, rather than only from the writer's own knowledge or experience. Writers of research reports must gather facts before they begin to write, and arrange their findings in a clear, concise, and useful form. Research reports are required in most subjects across the curriculum. The following research report about karate was written by a student.

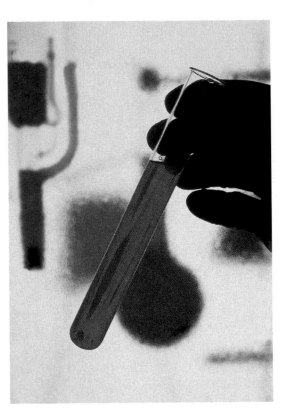

Learning Goals

- write a research report
- use subject-verb agreement correctly
- create a bibliography
- use transitions to connect ideas
- use apostrophes for possessives correctly

The Way of the Empty Hand

BY JILL PEACOCK

LINED UP IN ORDER OF RANK, THE STUDENTS KNEEL WITH their eyes closed. Their minds are becoming clear and focused. The teacher (sensei) tells them to open their eyes. With a swift bow, they are on their feet and ready to begin their class, to put meditation into motion. It is time to do karate.

Not only is karate fun, but it is good for the mind and the spirit. It can help you become a calmer person, improve your self-esteem, and get you into shape (Brimner 14). Sensei Michael Walsh, chief instructor at the Don Mills School of Karate, believes karate can help everybody in different ways. For example, it can help people let out their frustrations, and calm them down.

Thirteen-year-old Kimberley Young-Yow knows what Walsh means. He says practising kicking and punching with practice pads takes the edge off any stress he has. Karate puts his anger inside the practice pad and when he hits the pad, it goes away.

Walsh, who has a fifth-degree black belt, says karate can help young people focus and concentrate, which translates into better academic performance. For example, students who are initially afraid to answer questions in class gain confidence as their mental abilities improve through training and they may begin to excel at school.

The founding father of modern karate is considered to be Gichin Funakoshi. In 1903, Funakoshi demonstrated karate to the commissioner of an Okinawan school and it became part of the curriculum the following year. After that, the sensei set up the first dojo, or school (Lewis 12).

Although it originated on the Japanese island of Okinawa, karate has absorbed cultural influences from China and Southeast Asia. Various kicking techniques may have come from Thailand, whereas the open-handed fighting forms originated in China (Brimner 19). Early fighting skills such as the Egyptian bare-handed style and Japanese sumo wrestling may also have influenced the sport. Today, there are many different forms of karate.

Karate-do, which translates into "the way of the empty hand," uses a series of different coloured belts to show the student's rank (Walsh). White is the first belt and rating progresses through nine other belts, up to black. There are also nine possible degrees of black belt. The belt is worn around a traditional uniform, the gi, which is made of heavy cotton.

The sensei tests students to decide whether they are ready to move to the next level. Everyone who hopes to obtain a belt must attend a grading. This is a two- to three-hour test of skill, endurance, and strength. It is difficult physically and mentally. If a student passes, the new belt is ceremoniously wrapped around his or her waist.

One significant part of the grading is the kata. This is a series of self-defence movements put together to create an artistic demonstration of the technique. The techniques of movements get more difficult, and different stances are required as you progress through the different levels (Brimner 18).

Many participants find the kata fascinating because it looks similar to a dance but also has a practical aspect to it. When a student analyzes the kata and applies the movements, this is called bunkai. The bunkai is an essential part of learning and understanding the kata, and aids in making it more precise (Walsh).

In addition to using practice pads, karate students also participate in sparring as part of their training. With gloves and mouth guards, as well as head and foot protection, sparring gives the student a chance to practise in a realistic fighting environment. Sparring partners are only permitted to tap each other so there are no injuries. Compared to punching and kicking with practice pads, sparring is faster, utilizes more reflexes, and has most of the elements of a true fighting situation (Schroeder 105).

As karate students progress, they can begin to use weapons. These include tonfas, which are wooden and similar to a police officer's nightstick, seis (pronounced "sighs"), which look like a pair of miniature pitchforks because of their three prongs, and bows. Bows are long wooden staffs that have the thickness of a pool cue. These weapons are utilized during various advanced katas and self-defence routines (Metil 36).

Virtually anyone can start karate. As there are many different kinds, it is best to take a martial art that suits you. Judo comes from Japan and features many throwing techniques. Kung fu originated in China and includes movements based on the differing nature of particular animals. Aikido (the way of harmonized energy), concentrates on using the force created by an attacker against him, rather than focusing on a method of attack.

Another Japanese martial art is kendo. Called "the way of using the sword," it has developed over time from kenjutsu. The Japanese sword, which represents the soul of the warrior, only can be used to eliminate evil, never in anger.

The best way to find out more about a martial art is to contact a school nearby. Some centres give introductory classes for a low rate. Prior to signing up, keep in mind the purpose of karate. Walsh sums it up this way: "Karate combines mind, body, and spirit. Through it, you try to make your body stronger and healthier, your mind more capable of focusing, and your spirituality stronger. All the martial arts are meant to create balance and harmony within the person. The ultimate aim of karate is universal peace." ■

Bibliography

Brimner, Larry Dane. Karate. New York: Franklin Watts, 1988.

Lewis, Peter. Martial Arts of the Orient. London: Ward Lock, 1985.

Metil, Luana, and Jace Townsend. The Story of Karate: From Buddhism to Bruce Lee. Minneapolis, MN: Lerner Publications, 1995.

Schroeder, O.R., and Bill Wallace. Karate: Basic Concepts and Skills. Don Mills, ON: Addison-Wesley, 1987.

Walsh, Michael. Personal interview. 15 Dec. 1998.

Investigating the Model

1. The purpose of a research report is to present or summarize factual information (not your own opinion) about a topic in clear, concise, and accurate form. Find at least five facts about karate that appear in the model.

2. The introduction of a research report should catch the reader's interest and explain what the report is about. Determine how well the introduction of the model achieves these purposes. Who do you think the author intended as her audience?

3. The body of the report describes key information arranged into subtopics. Develop an outline containing the main headings the author might have used prior to writing her report. If you were writing the same report, would you have used the same order, or a different one? Why?

4. Reports are usually written in the third person (it, he, she), present tense, and in logical order. What exceptions to these general rules can you see in the model? How are they justified?

5. Depending on its topic and purpose, a research report may do the following:
    - compare
    - contrast
    - define
    - classify

    (For a definition of each of these terms, see page 207.) Find an example of each of these techniques in the model.

6. Any time you do research, you need to acknowledge your sources. A primary source is an interview, experiment, or observation you make yourself. Secondary sources are books, magazines, etc. that report information. Find examples in the text where the author used information from a primary source. What does this use of primary sources add to the style of the report?

Checkpoint: Research Report

 As a class, create a checklist of common features of research reports based on what you have just learned. You can use the checklist to help you write your own research report.

Writer's Workshop

1. Often, in school, you will be assigned a topic for a research report. If not, choose a topic that is of interest to both you and your audience. Make sure that you can cover the topic in no more than three typewritten pages and that there is enough information available on the subject.

2. Write a focus statement that highlights what your report is mainly going to be about; for example, "The point of my research is to inform other students about the benefits of karate." Notice that this statement also includes the purpose (inform) and audience (students) for the report. Your focus statement will not appear in your final report, but will serve as your guide as you do your research.

> **Learning Goal**
>
> • **write a research report**

3. Begin your research by consulting general resources, such as reading an encyclopedia article, browsing the Internet, or watching a television show on the subject, to get an overview of your topic. If you plan to do interviews, schedule them for later on, when you are more familiar with the topic and can ask better questions. Every time you consult a new article or book, write down all the information you will need for your bibliography. See pages 212–213 for some sample bibliographic entries. For a book, you need the following:
   - author's name
   - title of the book
   - publisher's name and the place of publication
   - date of publication

4. Once you are familiar enough with the general topic, make a list of three or four possible subtopics that you think your readers would find interesting (e.g., history of karate, weapons used). Write each of your subtopics on the top of a file card.

IDEA FILE

Possible sources of information include

- encyclopedias
- newspapers
- computer databases
- television shows
- field trips
- books
- magazines
- Internet
- interviews

5. To find information that fits your subtopics, you need to consult more specialized resources (i.e., read books that cover the topic in depth, interview people with expertise in the subject area, etc.) Each time you find a piece of information that fits one of your subtopics, write it on one of the cards. Some people prefer to write one piece of information on each card, while others use one card for several entries.

6. Write your notes in your own words, not in the words of the author. If you want to record an exact quotation, make sure you put quotation marks around the words and credit the author. (You may want to write direct quotations in a different coloured ink.)

7. When you think you have enough information, read through your cards and reject any facts or information that do not seem to fit the topic, or which you do not think are of interest. Lay all your remaining cards out on a flat surface, and rearrange them until you find a suitable order.

TECHNO-TIP

Use a computer to create file cards (records) of the information you wish to collect. This way the records can be reorganized electronically until you find the best order.

8. Write your first draft, including an introduction, body, and conclusion. Remember to begin a new paragraph for each subtopic.

✓ 9. Refer back to Checkpoint and revise your research report until you are satisfied with its focus, content, and organization. If necessary, do more research to make sure you have provided enough facts and examples for each subtopic. Prepare a bibliography, listing all the sources you used in your report. (See the Mechanics section for more information.)

Oral Language Extension

Working in groups of four or five, plan and present a multimedia documentary based on a research paper written by one of the members of the group. You may use computer graphics, visuals, props, demonstrations, videotaped or audiotaped interviews, music or sound effects to enhance your presentation. Remember to speak slowly and clearly, and to use facial expressions, gestures, and tone of voice to keep the audience interested.

Afterward, get feedback from the class as to how well your documentary or presentation came across. Aspects to consider when evaluating oral presentations or documentaries include clarity of speech, tone of voice, personal demeanour, interest level of the topic, flow of information, and the appropriate use of different media. Take note of suggestions that might improve your oral skills next time.

> **IDEA FILE**
>
> It's a good idea to get someone else to read your research report and give you their impressions. Ask your reader to highlight any sections that weren't clear, as well as pointing out parts that could be cut.

Grammar

Every sentence has a **subject** and a **verb**. A single subject takes a singular verb, and a plural subject takes a plural verb.

Making subjects and verbs agree in the past or future tenses is not a problem in English, because most verbs have the same form for all persons and numbers in these tenses (e.g., I, we went; I, you will go). However, because

Learning Goal

- use subject-verb agreement correctly

research reports are often written in the present tense, you may occasionally run into problems knowing which form of a verb to use. A quick review of some of the rules for subject-verb agreement may come in handy.

Note: For a review of subjects and predicates, see Unit 4.

- When the subject of a sentence consists of two or more singular nouns joined together by the word *and*, use a plural verb.

  Gloves and mouth guards **give** students a chance to practise in a realistic fighting environment.

- When a compound subject is linked by words such as *neither ... nor, either ... or,* make the verb agree with the part of the subject closest to the verb.

  Not only karate but also *judo and kendo* **come** from Japan.

- Collective nouns such as *family, group, crowd, army,* and *bunch* usually take a singular verb.

  The *class* **is** ready to put meditation into motion.
  BUT
  The *class* are putting on **their** uniforms.

- When the subject is separated from the verb by other words, make sure the verb agrees with the right word.

  Another of the martial arts **is** kendo.

WRITING TIP

Remember that the subject of the sentence is never found within a prepositional phrase, such as "of the martial arts."

- Indefinite pronouns ending in "one," "thing," and "body" always require a singular verb. So do *each, either, much,* and *neither.*

  Anyone **is** able to do karate.

- The indefinite pronouns *both, few, many, others,* and *several* take a plural verb.

  Many of the weapons **are** based on farming tools.

- The indefinite pronouns *all, any, more, most, none,* and *some* can be singular or plural, depending on what noun they refer to.

  Some of the <u>elements</u> of a real fight **exist** in sparring.
  BUT
  Some of the <u>grading</u> **depends** on the kata.

- Some nouns look plural, but are treated as singular (*mathematics, measles, physics, news, mumps,* and *economics*).

  Even *mathematics* **is** easier when you take karate!

1. The following sentences have been adapted from the model research report. Identify any errors in subject-verb agreement, and explain how you would fix them.
   a) Your mind, your body, and even your spirit all benefits from karate.
   b) Each of the martial arts have a different emphasis or technique.
   c) Either the tonfa, the sei, or the bow is used in advanced katas.
   d) The Japanese army have found that karate is excellent training for the military.
   e) The series of moves known as the kata are almost like a dance.
   f) None of the students are allowed to use their karate to hurt people, except in self-defence.
   g) Everyone in the class have to be willing to work hard.

2. Check through the research report that you wrote, and correct any errors you find in subject-verb agreement.

MEDIA LINK

Brainstorm a list of media-related jobs and choose one which you are interested in researching for an oral presentation. Prepare and present a research report that includes the following subtopics: a) origins of the profession and general background; b) training and education needed; c) changes in technology and future trends; and d) lifestyle. Rehearse your presentation several times before you present it to the class. You may use cue cards to remind you of what you want to say, but do not memorize your whole presentation word for word.

Mechanics

A **bibliography** is a list of books, articles, and other sources you used in your research. It not only shows readers where you got your information, but also enables readers to find these resources if they want to find out more about your topic.

Learning Goal

- create a bibliography

There are many different styles for writing bibliographies, so check with your teacher regarding his or her expectations. If your teacher has no preferred style, you may want to use the MLA (Modern Language Association) format, a standard style that is used in many schools. Examples of this style are found on pages 212–213.

In addition to a bibliography, your teacher may ask you to acknowledge your sources in the body of your report, in either a footnote or an in-text citation.

- Write **in-text citations** by putting in parentheses the author's last name and the page number(s) on which you found the information. Readers can then refer to the bibliography for the full source information. This reference is placed at the end of the last sentence or idea taken from the author.

  People take karate not only to get exercise, but also to improve their mind and spirit (Williams 68).

- Write **footnotes** by putting a small raised number at the end of the last sentence or idea taken from an author. Then, at the bottom of the page, write the number again, followed by all the information about the source, written as a single sentence. (If you refer to the same source in a later footnote, you can just write the author's name and the page number.)

  When writing footnotes, you do not have to reverse the author's name, and you can simply use a comma instead of a period between the author and the title of the work. The publication information goes in parentheses:

  Karate-do means "the way of the empty hand."[1]

  ---
  [1]Luana Metil and Jace Townsend, *The Story of Karate: From Buddhism to Bruce Lee* (Minneapolis, MN: Lerner Publications, 1995) 72.

1. Write a bibliography entry for this textbook, using MLA style or the style your teacher instructs you to use. Then write the same entry as a footnote. Compare your entries with that of a partner, and identify any differences. Make corrections if necessary.

2. Create bibliography references for imaginary sources making the entries as odd or as funny as you can. Then exchange the bibliography with a partner and correct any errors in each other's bibliographies.

3. Proofread the bibliography for your research paper carefully to make sure the format is correct.

Usage & Style

Transitions are words, phrases, or sentences that connect one idea with another.

When you write a research report, you want your ideas to build on each other and flow together. A list of transitions and their uses can be found on page 206 of this text.

Learning Goal

• use transitions to connect ideas

1. Find four examples of transitions in the model. Write these in your notebook. After each transition, indicate whether it is used to connect one idea to another within a paragraph or between paragraphs.

2. Working in pairs, choose any topic that might be used to write a research report. Take turns making oral statements about the topic. After the first statement, begin each statement with a transition word or phrase from the list on page 206.

1st student: Dogs provide companionship for people who are lonely.

2nd student: In addition, they can be useful in guarding against intruders.

1st student: Also, dogs provide blind people with access to their communities.

3. Reread your research report and look for places where you could connect ideas by adding transition words or phrases. Use the list on page 206 to help you find the best choice.

WORD ORIGINS

Karate (the way of the empty hand) is not the only word used in English that is borrowed from the Japanese. Look up the meaning and origin of each of the following words:

karaoke   tsunami   sushi   sayonara   kamikaze   tofu

Word Study & Spelling

Often, writers make mistakes when writing plurals and possessives. Examine each of the boldface words in the sentence groups below. The first sentence of each group comes from the model.

Learning Goal

- **use apostrophes for possessives correctly**

1. Explain the different spellings of the words in boldface below.
   a) Karate-do ... uses a series of different coloured belts to show the **student's** rank.
   b) **Students** are ranked on their ability to use weapons.
   c) **Students'** ranks range from the white belt through nine other belts to the black belt.

2. In groups of four, write at least four rules for forming plurals and possessives in nouns. Share them in some creative way with your classmates (i.e., a poster, brochure, rhyme, etc.). Use examples to clarify each rule.

3. Correct any errors in the use of plurals and possessives in the sentences below. Write the answers in your notebook.
   a) Kimberleys concentration improved after she started karate.
   b) The student's tests determined whether they were ready to move to the next level.

c) Sparring partners' are only permitted to tap each other so there are no injuries.

d) Some centre's give introductory classes for a low rate.

e) It's easy for anyone to enjoy karates' many benefits.

Looking Back

Before handing in your final draft, have a classmate check your research report, paying particular attention to the following:

 Do all verbs agree with their subjects, especially when the subject is compound, separated from the verb, or contains a collective noun or an indefinite article?

 Are there any nouns that look plural but should be treated as singular? If so, is the verb singular?

✓ Are sources cited in a bibliography or in footnotes? Are the citations written in a consistent style?

✓ Does the writer use transition words effectively to link ideas and paragraphs?

✓ Are plural and possessive nouns written properly?

TECHNO-TIP

 You can make your research report more clear on a computer by adding clip art, scanning photographs, or using a word processing or paint program to create diagrams, charts, or graphs.

Reflect and Build on Your Learning

Reflecting on Expository Writing Forms

1. Review the Learning Goals on page 113. Which goals do you think you have achieved most successfully? Which goals do you think will require you to do more work? Why?

2. This section covered three forms of exposition. What other forms of expository writing do you know? (You may wish to review the features of exposition on page 112.) Choose one of them and describe its features to a partner, explaining *why* and *when* you would use it. Does your partner agree with your explanation? Would you change anything you've said because of his or her feedback? In what way?

Looking Over Expository Writing Forms

1. Working with a small group, discuss what you know about explanations, précis, and research reports. To guide your discussion, create a chart that includes these three forms, as well as the additional form you chose for activity #2 above. Develop five criteria for comparing the forms. One criterion might be the purpose of each form. Complete the chart to compare the four forms. Compare your chart with those of other groups. How would you modify your chart based on what they have included in theirs?

CRITERIA	EXPLANATION	PRÉCIS	RESEARCH REPORT	OTHER
Purpose				

Using the Expository Writing Forms

1. What are the forms of exposition used in your school subjects? How does knowledge of the features of these forms help make you a better reader and writer in these subjects? From what you learned in this section, what would you change about how you currently read and write exposition?

2. Working with a small group, write a set of instructions on chart paper for an audience of ten- or eleven-year-olds on how to use a Web search engine to find information. Make sure to choose a topic that would be of interest to this audience, and include visual illustrations such as Web site maps if necessary. Revise your instructions so that your audience will easily follow them. Carefully edit and proofread the instructions, especially for the checklist of items on page 125. Display and present your instructions to the class. Revise them based on class feedback.

3. Find an example of explanation in one of your favourite short stories, novels, or plays. For readers also familiar with the work, write a short essay on the accuracy and significance of the explanation. To help focus and organize your essay, consider such questions as: What is being explained and how important is the explanation to the development of the plot? Is the explanation presented in the first or third person? How reliable is the source presenting the explanation? Make sure your essay has a main point, with connecting words to help unify the information and ideas you are presenting for your readers.

4. Write a research report on the jargon, or specialized language, of a particular area (e.g., computers), or on the origins of English words from another language such as Latin or Arabic. Locate and summarize information from resources such as dictionaries, encyclopedia articles, interviews, and the Internet, organizing the information into interesting subtopics. When you write your report, provide an introduction, body, conclusion, and a brief bibliography. Ask a classmate to check a complete draft of your report to make sure that it is interesting to readers, well organized, and provides enough facts and examples for each subtopic. Revise your report as needed, and have your classmate edit and proofread it carefully, especially for the checklist of items on page 153.

5. Exchange a research report or short essay with a partner. Read your partner's report or essay carefully, then write a précis of it, using as a guide the class checklist of précis features. Read each other's précis and make constructive suggestions for improvement based on the checklist.

BUILD ON YOUR LEARNING

Persuasion

Persuasive writing is writing with a purpose. It is writing that moves readers to believe or to act through logic, argument, or emotional appeals. Whether you are trying to persuade government officials to clean up an environmental hazard or to convince a consumer that your product is the best choice, persuasive writing is an effective means of getting your message heard.

This section contains three very different persuasive forms of writing: comparison, advertisement, and letter to the editor. Each achieves its purpose using logical and emotional arguments that are suited to a specific audience.

Features of Persuasion

- Persuasive writing aims to move the reader to support a point of view or to act in support of an idea or cause.
- A persuasive piece often begins with a statement of the author's position, then presents arguments and evidence in favour of that position, and concludes with a call to action or a recommendation.
- Persuasive writers arrange their points for maximum impact on their audience.
- Persuasion usually uses a combination of logical and emotional appeals designed to win over a specific audience.

Learning Goals

- use print and electronic sources to gather information and explore ideas for your written work

- identify and use informational forms appropriately in writing a comparison, an advertisement, and a letter to the editor

- use organizational techniques to present ideas and supporting details

- revise your written work independently and collaboratively

- edit and proofread to produce final drafts using correct grammar, spelling, and punctuation

- use knowledge of vocabulary and language conventions; for example, identify and correct sentence fragments

- develop listening, speaking, and media literacy skills

- read a variety of nonfiction, such as comparison, advertisement, and letter to the editor

- identify and understand the elements and style of a variety of nonfiction

Unit 10 Comparison

What is a comparison?

A comparison is a powerful writing technique used in all subjects across the curriculum to identify similarities and differences between or among two or more people, places, actions, or things. Comparisons may be descriptive, expository, or persuasive. Their purpose may be to analyze, differentiate, define, explain, evaluate, inform, persuade—or even to entertain, as the following essay illustrates.

Learning Goals

- write a comparison
- use comparative and superlative forms of adjectives and adverbs correctly
- use colons, semicolons, and dashes correctly
- recognize and correct errors in comparison sentences
- learn to use homophones correctly

Neat People vs. Sloppy People

BY SUZANNE BRITT

I'VE FINALLY FIGURED OUT THE DIFFERENCE BETWEEN NEAT people and sloppy people. The distinction is, as always, moral. Neat people are lazier and meaner than sloppy people.

Sloppy people, you see, are not really sloppy. Their sloppiness is merely the unfortunate consequence of their extreme moral rectitude. Sloppy people carry in their mind's eye a heavenly vision, a precise plan, that is so stupendous, so perfect, it can't be achieved in this world or the next.

Sloppy people live in Never-Never Land. Someday is their metier. Someday they are planning to alphabetize all their books and set up home catalogs. Someday they will go through their wardrobes and mark certain items for tentative mending and certain items for passing on to relatives of similar shape and size. Someday sloppy people will make a family scrapbook into which they will put newspaper clippings, postcards, locks of hair, and the dried corsage from their senior prom. Someday they will file everything on the surface of their desks, including the cash receipts from coffee purchases at the snack shop. Someday they will sit down and read all the back issues of *The New Yorker.*

For all these noble reasons and more, sloppy people never get neat. They aim too high and wide. They save everything, planning someday to file, order, and straighten out the world. But while these ambitious plans take clearer and clearer shape in their heads, the books spill from the shelves onto the floor, the clothes pile up in the hamper and the closet, the family mementos accumulate in every drawer, the surface of the desk is buried under mounds of paper, and the unread magazines threaten to reach the ceiling.

Sloppy people can't bear to part with anything. They give loving attention to every detail. When sloppy people say they're going to tackle the surface of the desk, they really mean it. Not a paper will go unturned; not a rubber band will go unboxed. Four hours or two weeks into the excavation, the desk looks exactly the same, primarily because the sloppy person is meticulously creating new piles of papers with new headings and scrupulously stopping to read all the old book catalogs before he throws them away. A neat person would just bulldoze the desk.

Neat people are bums and clods at heart. They have cavalier attitudes toward possessions, including family heirlooms. Everything is just another dust-catcher to them. If anything collects dust, it's got to go and that's that.

Neat people will toy with the idea of throwing the children out of the house just to cut down on the clutter.

Neat people don't care about process. They like results. What they want to do is get the whole thing over with so they can sit down and watch the rasslin' on TV. Neat people operate on two unvarying principles: Never handle any item twice, and throw everything away.

The only thing messy in a neat person's house is the trash can. The minute something comes to a neat person's hand, he will look at it, try to decide if it has immediate use, and, finding none, throw it in the trash.

Neat people are especially vicious with mail. They never go through their mail unless they are standing directly over a trash can. If the trash can is beside the mailbox, even better. All ads, catalogs, pleas for charitable contributions, church bulletins, and money-saving coupons go straight into the trash can without being opened. All letters from home, postcards from Europe, bills and paychecks are opened, immediately responded to, then dropped in the trash can. Neat people keep their receipts only for tax purposes. That's it. No sentimental salvaging of birthday cards or the last letter a dying relative ever wrote. Into the trash it goes.

Neat people place neatness above everything, even economics. They are incredibly wasteful. Neat people throw away several toys every time they walk through the den. I knew a neat person once who threw away a perfectly good dish drainer because it had mold on it. The drainer was too much trouble to wash. And neat people sell their furniture when they move. They will sell a La-Z-Boy recliner while you are reclining in it.

Neat people are no good to borrow from. Neat people buy everything in expensive little single portions. They get their flour and sugar in two-pound bags. They wouldn't consider clipping a coupon, saving a leftover, reusing plastic nondairy whipped cream containers or rinsing off tin foil and draping it over the unmoldy dish drainer. You can never borrow a neat person's newspaper to see what's playing at the movies. Neat people have the paper all wadded up and in the trash by 7:05 a.m.

Neat people cut a clean swath through the organic as well as the inorganic world. People, animals, and things are all one to them. They are so insensitive. After they've finished with the pantry, the medicine cabinet, and the attic, they will throw out the red geranium (too many leaves), sell the dog (too many fleas), and send the children off to boarding school (too many scuff marks on the hardwood floors). ■

Investigating the Model

1. Comparisons are used in descriptive, expository, or persuasive writing to examine two or more subjects. Suzanne Britt's purpose in writing was to persuade the audience through humour that being messy is superior to being neat. As a class, discuss how this purpose affects the way she presents her comparison (e.g., word choice, organization, content). Use evidence from the text to back up your answer.

2. Points for comparison may be based on direct observation, analysis, or research. On what basis does the author of the model make her comparison? Is it a valid basis? How would this piece of writing be different if the basis for comparison was research?

3. Like most forms of nonfiction, a comparison should contain a thesis sentence that limits the scope of the comparison and reveals its purpose. Find the thesis statement in the model. Then choose four paragraphs from the body of the piece and show how they relate to the thesis.

4. Comparisons are usually organized in one of two ways:
   The Block Method (AA, BB): Arranged by subject. All characteristics of

Subject A are discussed first, followed by all characteristics of Subject B. This method works best with short comparisons.

The Point-by-Point Method (AB, AB): Arranged by characteristics. One characteristic of Subject A is discussed, then it is compared with the same characteristic in Subject B. This approach is better for longer comparisons, and when the purpose is to define one or the other of the two subjects.

Which of these methods does Suzanne Britt use? Why do you think she chose this method over the other?

5. A comparison may include both the common elements of and the distinctions between or among the topics being compared. Sometimes, however, the author's purpose is better served if the comparison focuses exclusively on either the similarities or the differences. What approach has Suzanne Britt taken in her piece? How does this approach relate to her purpose?

6. Since comparisons are often part of longer pieces of writing, they do not always have conclusions. However, in comparisons that stand alone, the conclusion usually summarizes, evaluates, or draws a conclusion based on the points mentioned in the body of the piece. What do you think of the conclusion of the model comparison? How else might the piece have ended?

Checkpoint: Comparison

✓ As a class, create a checklist of common features of comparisons, based on what you have just learned. You can use the checklist to help you write your own comparison.

Writer's Workshop

Learning Goal

- **write a comparison**

1. As a class, brainstorm possible topics for a comparison of two characters, places, actions, or things. Choose subjects that are similar in some way, but not completely the same. Your intention should be to persuade your audience that one or the other subject is superior.

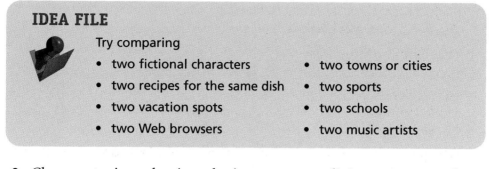

IDEA FILE

Try comparing

- two fictional characters
- two recipes for the same dish
- two vacation spots
- two Web browsers
- two towns or cities
- two sports
- two schools
- two music artists

2. Choose a topic, and write a thesis statement outlining your reason for writing. Since this is a persuasive piece, your purpose should include a word like "convince," "persuade," or "evaluate." For example, "I am writing to convince my readers that sloppy people are morally superior to neat people."

Note: For a list of key words and their meanings, see pages 207–208.

3. Make a Venn diagram (two circles that overlap). In the left-hand segment (A), list information about the first item being compared. In the right-hand segment (B), list information about the second item being compared. In the section where both circles overlap (C), list features that both items have in common.

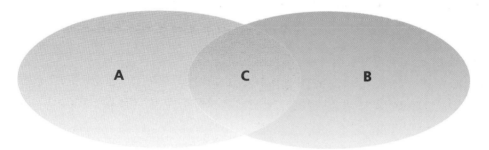

4. Put a check mark beside at least five points you think are significant. If you have fewer than five similarities or differences you need to do further observation, analysis, or research.

5. Number the details in your Venn diagram in the order that you wish to write about them. Often, it makes sense to begin with a fairly strong

point to hook your audience, put weaker points in the middle where they won't be as obvious, and end with your strongest argument to leave readers convinced.

6. Decide whether you will use the block method or the point-by-point method to organize your comparison (see Investigating the Model).

7. Write your comparison. Include a concluding comment.

☑ 8. Refer back to the list you created at Checkpoint, and revise and edit your comparison until you are satisfied with its focus, content, and organization.

Oral Language Extension

Work with four or five other students to create a list of do's and don'ts for working in groups. Plan a role-play that illustrates a group that is functioning poorly, including as many examples from your don't list as possible. Present your scene to the class, and invite the audience to identify the problems they noticed and suggest solutions. As other groups present their role-plays, take notes on problems you identify, so you can discuss them after the performance.

Use all of the group lists to create a chart entitled "The Do's and Don'ts of Group Behaviour." Post this list in the class for reference.

Grammar

Form the **comparative** of an adjective or adverb by adding -*er* to the root word; for longer words, use *more* before the root word instead of the -*er* suffix. Form the **superlative** by adding -*est* to the root, or by inserting the word *most* before the word.

Learning Goal

- **use comparative and superlative forms of adjectives and adverbs correctly**

One-syllable adjectives and adverbs usually add -*er* and -*est* to form the comparative and superlative degrees; those with two or more syllables sometimes add -*er* and -*est*, but most of them add the words *more* and *most*. If you are unsure what form to use, consult a dictionary.

	Positive	Comparative	Superlative
Adjectives	old	older	oldest
	careful	more careful	most careful
Adverbs	sloppy	sloppier	sloppiest
	slowly	more slowly	most slowly

Use the **superlative** (neatest, most carefully) only when there are more than two subjects.

Some common words have irregular comparative and/or superlative forms. These forms do not follow any rules; they have to be memorized.

good	better	best
bad	worse	worst
little	less	least
some	more	most

When only two subjects are being compared, always use the comparative form.

Wrong: The author prefers sloppy people to those who are neat, because sloppy people are the *nicest* and *most* thoughtful group.

Right: The author prefers sloppy people to those who are neat, because sloppy people are the *nicer* and *more* thoughtful group.

Never use *more* (or *less*) with an *-er* ending, or *most* (or *least*) with an *-est* ending. This forms a double comparison.

Wrong: The **most friendliest** person I ever met was even **more messier** than I am.

Right: The **friendliest** person I ever met was even **messier** than I am.

1. Rewrite the following passage, correcting any errors in comparative or superlative form.

   Most people think that being neat is more better than being messy, but Suzanne Britt has a different idea. She believes that neat people are the most meanest of the two personality types, and that the sloppier you are, the gooder you are. Britt may be more well informed that I, but in my experience we neat people are most likely to have time to be nice. Unlike sloppy people, we get the more boringer work out of the way so we can concentrate on helping others. Besides, neat people are the least likeliest of all people to "watch the rasslin' on TV" because we could never stand to see all those bodies littering the ring!

2. Write five sentences of your own comparing neat people and sloppy people. Use the correct comparative or superlative forms of adjectives or adverbs in each sentence.

MEDIA LINK

Compare the front pages of three daily newspapers published on the same day. Analyze the layouts (colour, typeface, images, captions, headlines, amount of written copy and visual material), as well as the treatment of the lead story and the number and placement of other stories. Based on your analysis, identify the strengths and weaknesses of each front page, and describe the target reader for each newspaper. Summarize your findings in an oral report.

Mechanics

Colons, semicolons, and **dashes** can all be used to join two related ideas. Knowing how to use these punctuation marks will help you add some variety to your comparisons.

Use a **colon** to draw attention to the words that come after it.

These words may be a list, or a restatement or description of something before the colon. The words before the colon must be a complete thought.

Wrong: Someday sloppy people will make a family scrapbook containing: newspaper clippings, postcards, locks of hair, and the dried corsage from their senior prom.

Right: Someday sloppy people will make a family scrapbook containing the following: newspaper clippings, postcards, locks of hair, and the dried corsage from their senior prom.

1. Find at least three passages from the model that could be reworded using a colon followed by a list or a restatement. Present the new versions to a partner and discuss which wording you like better: yours or that of the model.

> **Learning Goal**
>
> • **use colons, semicolons, and dashes correctly**

Use a **semicolon** to indicate that two main clauses are closely related.

Not a paper will go unturned; not a rubber band will go unboxed.

WRITING TIP

Note that what comes after the colon does not have to be a complete clause, but what comes after a semicolon does.

Use a semicolon before adverbs like *however, nevertheless, moreover, therefore, in fact,* or *for example,* but not before coordinating conjunctions (*and, or, nor, for, but, so, yet*); since the conjunction already coordinates the two clauses it joins, the use of the semicolon is excessive.

Sloppy people live in Never-Never Land; for example, they swear that someday they will go through their wardrobes, **but** they never, never will.

2. Decide whether each of the following comparisons requires a colon or a semicolon.

   a) Neat people are worse than sloppy people in two ways_ they are lazier and meaner.

   b) A neat person uses a three-step process for everything_ he will look at it, try to decide if it has immediate use, and, finding none, throw it in the trash.

   c) A common theme runs through all these examples_ it is better to be too sloppy than too neat.

   d) Neat people don't care about process_ however, they like results.

   e) There is only one messy thing in a neat person's house_ the trash can.

   f) Neat people are incredibly wasteful_ on the other hand, messy people can't bear to part with anything.

WRITING TIP

In all of the sentences above, a **dash** could have replaced the colon or semicolon. However, use dashes sparingly, when you want to place extra emphasis on particular words. They encourage disjointed writing and are not as precise as a colon or semicolon.

Usage & Style

Than is a conjunction used in comparisons; **then** is an adverb denoting time.

Neat people are lazier and meaner than sloppy people.

All letters from home, postcards from Europe, bills and paychecks are opened, immediately responded to, then dropped in a trash can.

Different from is ordinarily used in comparisons. However, **different than** is acceptable to avoid an awkward construction.

A neat person is different from a sloppy person.

Please let me know if your room and closet are different than they were yesterday.

Differ from means "to be unlike"; **differ with** means "to disagree."

A neat person's approach to the mail differs from that of a sloppy person.

My mother differed with me about the meaning of the word "neat."

1. Correct any usage problems in the following comparisons. Write the correct answers in your notebook. If a sentence does not have a problem, write the word "correct" instead.

Learning Goal

- **recognize and correct errors in comparison sentences**

   a) How does my desk differ with your vision of what a desk should look like?
   b) Linda is much neater then Rhoda.
   c) "I beg to differ from you," she replied.
   d) I've finally figured out how neat people are different than sloppy people.
   e) Sloppy people carry in their mind's eye a view that is different from neat people.
   f) Your ideas about attention to detail are different than mine.
   g) I differ than you on several points.

Words like **different** and **unique** have no comparative or superlative.

Wrong: British Columbia is more different from other provinces because it has the most unique landscapes.

Right: British Columbia is different from other provinces because it has unique landscapes.

Use **few, fewer**, and **fewest** for things that can be counted; use **little, less**, or **least** for quantities that cannot be counted.

There are fewer sloppy people than neat people.

My desk is less cluttered than yours.

2. Correct any errors in the use of comparisons in the following paragraph.

In my opinion, sloppy people are more cool than neat people. For one thing, they are the most entertaining because you never know how they will manage things. Neat people are less likelier to try something new; rather, their approach to life is more predictable. While both types of people are, in their own way, more different, sloppy people are most sharp when it comes to saving something valuable. While neat people spend littler time saving things, sloppy people savour the time spent organizing their piles of clutter. Also, neat people spend less hours at important tasks.

Word Study & Spelling

The English language contains many troublesome word pairs (or triplets) that are often confused because they look or sound alike. Many of these are homophones—words that sound alike, but have different meanings and spellings.

Learning Goal

- **learn to use homophones correctly**

1. Each of the words below, all taken from the model, are often confused with one or more other words. Write the troublesome word partner (or partners) that should accompany each word and then write sentences to clarify their meaning.

Example: *manor/manner* You could tell by her manner that she was raised in a manor.

a) to	**b)** see	**c)** which
d) mail	**e)** through	**f)** their
g) buy	**h)** knew	**i)** whole

TECHNO-TIP

If you rely on a spell-check program to correct your spelling mistakes, be aware that troublesome word pairs will fool any spell-checking program: as long as the word is a real word, the computer can't tell that you have misspelled it.

One way to differentiate homophones is to associate each word with others that have similar meanings and spelling patterns. For instance,

to **to**ward in**to** **to**gether

two **tw**ice **tw**in **tw**elve **tw**enty

2. List words with similar meanings and spelling patterns for five of the troublesome word groups you identified in activity #1.

A further list of commonly misused words is found on pages 208–210 of this textbook. Read the list so you know which words are covered. Then refer to the list whenever necessary during your writing.

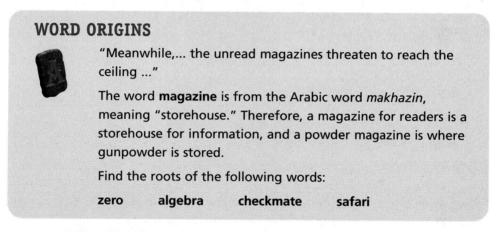

WORD ORIGINS

"Meanwhile,... the unread magazines threaten to reach the ceiling ..."

The word **magazine** is from the Arabic word *makhazin*, meaning "storehouse." Therefore, a magazine for readers is a storehouse for information, and a powder magazine is where gunpowder is stored.

Find the roots of the following words:

zero **algebra** **checkmate** **safari**

Looking Back

Before handing in your final edited draft, have a classmate check your comparison, paying particular attention to the following:

 Are all comparisons using adjectives or adverbs written correctly?

 Are colons, semicolons, and dashes used correctly and appropriately?

 Has the author used expressions such as *different from, differ from/with*, and *few/less* correctly?

 Are all words spelled correctly?

Unit 11 Advertisement

What is an advertisement?

An advertisement is usually meant to sell a product, create an image, or promote a company or brand name. Effective advertising catches your attention by direct, simply worded text and compelling visuals designed to appeal to a particular audience. The form of an advertisement depends on the purpose, the target audience, and the medium in which it appears. The models presented here include two print advertisements and an excerpt from a Web page.

Learning Goals

- write an advertisement
- identify and correct sentence fragments
- identify design elements
- adapt punctuation for advertisements
- identify and explain examples of slang and colloquialisms
- use knowledge of useful spelling rules

Netscape: Milk - All About Milk - Nutrient Knowledge

| Back | Forward | Home | Edit | Reload | Images | Print | Find | Stop |

Location : http://www.whymilk.com/about/nutrient/index.html

| What's New? | What's Cool? | Destinations | Net Search | People | Software |

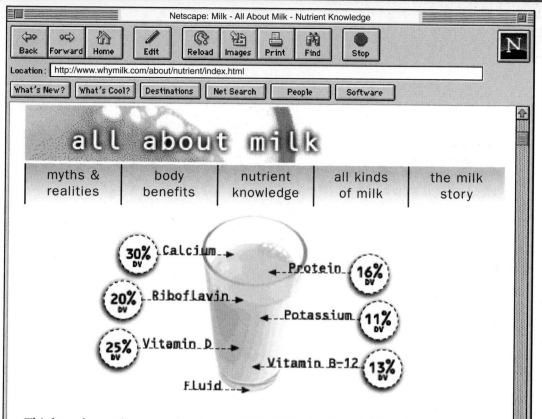

all about milk

| myths & realities | body benefits | nutrient knowledge | all kinds of milk | the milk story |

Think you're getting enough calcium? Well, 85% of girls and 60% of guys aren't! Calcium is one of the most essential bone-growin' nutrients, and milk is one of the best sources in the natural world for calcium. Be sure to visit the <u>Personal Trainer</u> and check your Calcium Quotient to make sure your bod isn't suffering from milk thirst.

Also, with all of us protecting ourselves from the sun more and more, we might be missing out on one important thing (no, not a great tan). Vitamin D! Guess where you can get the D without the burn? Give you a clue—it starts with M-I-L—OK, OK, we know you're not stupid. Just make sure to drink at least three cups of milk a day and prove us right.

For more surprising facts about milk, call 1-800-WHY-MILK (1-800-949-6455) 24 hours a day, 7 days a week, <u>e-mail us</u>, or let us send you some of our free fact-packed <u>brochures</u>. We'll be happy to give you more information on the topics covered in this Web site or answers to any other questions you may have about milk.

Document: Done.

Drink Milk. Love Life.

Investigating the Models

1. Advertisements are designed to sell a particular product or service, create an image, provide information, or persuade an audience to behave in a certain way. Identify the main purpose for the print ad and the Web page excerpt.

2. Advertisements are almost always targeted at a particular audience. Advertisers hope to appeal to their audiences through the images, language, associations, and overall tone of their ads. Who do you think the milk ad and Web site are targeting?

3. Advertisements usually rely on a combination of words and images to convey their message. Which of the models relies more on text? Which relies more on images? Why do you think this is so?

4. The medium in which an ad appears affects its style and its content. Identify the difference in content and presentation between the milk Web page and the milk ad. What other differences do you notice? Identify some physical or technological limitations of print ads and of Web pages that might also have an influence on what they contain.

5. Like poems, ads often break grammatical rules in order to increase the impact of their message or create a strong image. For example, they may use single words, fragments, or short phrases as sentences. Choose three examples of wording from the models that you think are particularly powerful.

6. Some advertisements are designed to promote the product directly by pointing out its features, price, etc. Other advertisements sell the product indirectly, often by associating it with some desirable image or quality (for example, heightened experience, acceptance and popularity,

health and attractiveness, financial success, exclusive membership), or by associating the product with high-profile people. What associations do the models make with their products? Which approach do you think is more effective? Why?

Checkpoint: Advertisement

✓ As a class, create a checklist of common features of advertisements, based on what you have just learned. You can use the checklist to help you create your own advertisement.

Writer's Workshop

1. Working in groups of four, brainstorm a list of products or services for which you would like to write both a print ad and a Web page. If possible, think of a product or service that would appeal to people your age. You could choose something you have seen advertised elsewhere, or you may choose to make something up.

Learning Goal

* **write an advertisement**

2. Two of you will work on the Web page, and two of you will create a magazine ad. Since you cannot write a whole Web site, concentrate on creating a page that includes information about your product, as does the Web page for milk on page 173. Your print advertisement should be aimed at creating an image for your product; your Web page will provide background information. Decide as a group what you will include in each form of advertising, and how you will differentiate them.

IDEA FILE

Working as a class, make a list of effective Web sites that members of your class have visited. Also, check in the resource centre of your school for directories of Web sites. Visit those Web sites that may provide you with some suitable topics for your writing.

3. Prepare a profile of your target audience, listing their age, gender, income range, interests, and educational level, along with other characteristics you think are important.

4. Make a point-form list of the information you want to get across to your target audience. Decide what information to include in your print ad and what to include in your Web page.

5. Working with your partner on either the print ad or the Web page, consider what illustrations or backgrounds might work to create a suitable image for your product or service. Consider how you will use these images, bearing in mind the limitations of your medium.

WRITING TIP

Don't overuse graphics on a Web page; readers may get frustrated if the images take too long to download. Similarly, too much writing in a print ad will make readers turn the page.

6. Write the copy for your print ad or Web page, using language that will appeal to your target audience.

7. Format your text by hand or on a computer, using different fonts, type sizes, graphics, and other techniques to emphasize key words and concepts.

8. Exchange your work with the other two members of your original team, and get their feedback. Do the two types of advertising complement each other? What changes can you make to content or style that will improve them?

9. Use the list you developed at Checkpoint to revise your ad and web page.

Oral Language Extension

Your class has been hired to create a radio ad campaign to promote oral communication skills to students in your school. Each ad in the series will focus on how these skills are useful in one particular subject area (e.g., English, mathematics, physical education).

Working in groups of three or four, arrange an interview with a teacher, and prepare some specific questions about the importance of both listening and speaking skills in his or her subject area. (Be sure to check with other groups to make sure you are not interviewing the same teacher.) Record the interview, so you can include parts of it in your broadcast. Plan and tape the commercial, making sure it is no more than 30 seconds long. Consider using music, sound effects, or interview clips to get your audience's attention. Pay close attention to the clarity of your speech and the tone of your voice as you tape the ad.

If your school has a PA system, ask if you can play one commercial a day during announcements.

Grammar

A **sentence fragment** is a group of words that looks like a sentence, but instead is just an incomplete thought. In many sentence fragments, either a subject or a verb or both are missing.

1. Identify whether the following groups of words are sentences (S) or sentence fragments (F). Rewrite the sentence fragments to make them into sentences.
   a) Just do it.
   b) Drink Milk.
   c) Looking Great!
   d) In a class by itself.
   e) Vitamin D!
   f) Fitness for your face.

Note: For more on faulty sentence structure, see Unit 4.

WRITING TIP

While sentence fragments are often used in everyday speech, they are seldom acceptable in writing. They may be used in writing to

- create effect in advertising, poetry, or fiction
- write dialogue, which is really conversation
- take notes
- record the answer to a question

Here are some types of sentence fragments to watch out for in your writing:

- subordinate clauses on their own

    Sentence fragment: Because it's good for you.

    Complete sentence: Drink milk because it's good for you.

- phrases on their own

    Sentence fragment: From here to there, pronto.

    Complete sentence: We'll get your package from here to there, pronto.

- Sentences beginning with a coordinating conjunction (*and, but, or, so, yet*). While starting a sentence with a coordinating conjunction is acceptable in informal writing, it is technically wrong, since the coordinating conjunction is meant to connect two main clauses. Do not use this construction in more formal writing.

Learning Goal

- **identify and correct sentence fragments**

    Sentence fragment: So the next time you need help, just call us.

    Complete sentence: The next time you need help, call us.

2. Rewrite the sentence fragments below to make them sentences, or combine them with the other sentence on the same line to make one complete sentence.
    a) You deserve the best. So be good to yourself.
    b) We know that this cream will cleanse your skin. Deep down.
    c) Good things will happen. If you drink milk.

d) Apply it at night. And wake up refreshed.

e) Do it. Because you owe it to yourself.

3. Collect sentence fragments from advertisements you see in print or on TV. Share your examples with the class, and discuss how the sentence fragments help to create a mood or image in the advertisement.

4. Although it is acceptable to use sentence fragments in some instances, you should use them intentionally, rather than unintentionally. Review your ad or web page copy. Are there any sentence fragments? If so, did you use them on purpose? Explain your reason for using sentence fragments, and change any that you feel are not justified.

MEDIA LINK

Keep a log for a 24-hour period of your exposure to advertising. Note what is being advertised and where the advertisement appeared. Include ads from all sources: billboards, posters, buses, clothing, cereal packages, screen savers, T-shirts, logos, etc., as well as radio, television, and print. Summarize your results, highlighting the total number of ads you were exposed to, as well as any interesting patterns that emerged (e.g., how many ads were aimed at a teen market, which medium predominated, etc.). To what degree do you think you are influenced by these advertisements?

Mechanics

No matter what medium they are working in, designers use certain standard techniques to capture and direct your eyes to key information, and to convey mood and attitude. Here are a few features to watch for in advertisements.

Learning Goal

- **identify design elements**

- Designers use different **fonts** (typefaces) to convey their message.

- The **size of the type** also helps to emphasize key words and ideas.

- As important as the writing or the graphics is the use of **white space**. Not enough blank space gives a cramped feeling.

- To emphasize certain words and draw attention to them, designers may use **bold** or **italic type**.

- To make numerical data more easily understood, designers may use **visual aids** such as charts and graphs.

- **Colour** is another important way that designers draw our attention.

- **Boxes, bullets,** and **underlining** help to set apart lists and important information.

1. Working in groups of four, examine each of the three models and assess their design using the list of features above. Discuss how each of the features identified contributes to the meaning and organization of the ad.

TECHNO-TIP

Most word processing programs have several typefaces from which to choose. While there are no hard and fast rules about the kind of typefaces that must be used in given situations, formal typefaces (e.g., Times) usually attribute importance to a subject, while informal typefaces often suggest a more relaxed atmosphere. What do the following typefaces suggest to you?

> Drink Milk. Love Life.
> Drink Milk. Love Life.
> *Drink Milk. Love Life.*

---

2. **a)** These design features apply not only to ads but to other texts as well. Assess the design of this textbook and of a textbook you are using in another class, using the list of features above.

   b) List other features that textbooks often include to help highlight important information.

Learning Goal

- adapt punctuation for advertisements

Sometimes, punctuation is used in advertising to provide emphasis. Questions and exclamations are used frequently in person-to-person communication. Advertisers use this type of punctuation to involve you personally.

3. Each of the sentences below is taken from one of the models. Explain how the punctuation used in each sentence catches your attention, involves you, or gets you to read further.

   a) Think you're getting enough calcium?

   b) Vitamin D!

   c) Be sure to visit the Personal Trainer....

   d) Drink Milk. Love Life.

4. Use the information you learned about advertising layout in this section to make changes to your advertisement.

Usage & Style

Advertisers know that there are different levels of language, and they are careful to use the types of phrases and expressions that are most likely to appeal to their target audience or create the desired mood.

> **Standard Canadian English** follows widely accepted rules of grammar, usage, and mechanics. **Nonstandard Canadian English** consists of all the dialects of English spoken in the world.

Standard Canadian English can be formal or informal, depending on the situation and audience.

1. For each of the following sentences, identify the language as being either standard or nonstandard.

   a) Give you a clue—it starts with M-I-L—OK, OK, we know you're not stupid.

   b) I ain't foolin': it's great!

   c) Just make sure to drink at least three cups of milk a day and prove us right.

   d) That rush. That adrenaline.

   e) Drinking milk makes good sense.

Colloquialisms are words and phrases used in informal language but inappropriate in formal language or speech (e.g., "What's happening?", "Take five," and "goofing

> ### Learning Goal
> - identify and explain examples of slang and colloquialisms

around"). Authors use colloquial language in dialogue to make the language sound natural.

2. Make a list of three colloquial expressions used in everyday speech. Use each of them in a sentence; then share your sentences with your classmates.

Slang is language used by a particular group of people. It is a highly informal language that sometimes only the group of people using it can understand. It is usually spoken. Words and expressions are added and dropped frequently, so writers seldom use it. Advertisers, however, love it. Examples of slang from different eras include "razz," "diss," and "jive."

Note: For information on dialect, see Unit 3.

3. Look through magazines to find examples of ads that use slang expressions. What effect does this use of language have? What audience is the advertiser hoping to attract?

4. Identify two other slang expressions that teenagers currently use, and two that have gone out of favour. Compare your examples with those of others in the class, and create a class dictionary of slang.

5. Check your advertisement to make sure that the level of language used is appropriate to your purpose and your audience.

Word Study & Spelling

English has many rules for spelling. Here are five of the most useful.

Learning Goal

- use knowledge of useful spelling rules

- Use *i* before *e* except after *c* or when it sounds like *a* as in *neighbour* and *weigh*.

niece	achieve	grieve	relieve
BUT			
receive	ceiling	eight	freight

- When a *c* at the beginning of a word is followed by *e, i,* or *y,* it is soft (says *s*); otherwise, it is hard (says *k*).

city	circus	cement	cemetery	cyst	Cyprus

  BUT

capital	clock	collapse	custody

- Words ending in a consonant plus *y* change the *y* to *i* before adding a suffix other than *ing*.

marry	married	marrying
worry	worrier	worrying

- Drop the silent *e* from a root word before adding *ing*.

make	making
cope	coping

- For one-syllable words with a short vowel, double the final consonant before adding an ending.

mat	matting	matted
win	winner	winning
hop	hopping	hopped

1. **a)** Find at least one example from the models to illustrate each of these five rules.
   b) Think up three more examples for each rule. Mix the words, and dictate them to a classmate. Check the spelling of your classmate's words.

2. Unfortunately, just as there are many rules for spelling in English, there are also many exceptions to those rules. With a partner, try to think of a word that does not follow one of these rules. Compare your word with those of others in the class, and compile a list of exceptions to be posted in the classroom.

WORD ORIGINS

Advertisers usually go out of their way to encourage people to associate their brand name with a particular product. But occasionally they are so successful that the brand name itself changes from a proper noun to a common noun or verb. When a trade name is debased in this way, it loses its value, because any other company can use it. **Photostat, laundromat, rayon, nylon, escalator,** and **celluloid** are all former brand names that have met this fate. Others are still registered as trademarks (and so should be used with care), but are in danger of becoming debased. For example, we often refer informally to tissues as **Kleenexes,** and to bandages as **Band-Aids,** whether or not they bear the actual Kleenex or Band-Aid brand names.

With a partner, think of other brand names that are used in this way. Suggest a more generic (i.e., general) term that could be used to replace the brand name.

Looking Back

Before handing in your final edited draft, have a classmate check your advertisement, paying particular attention to the following:

 Are there sentence fragments used? If so, are they used in appropriate situations?

 Are the levels of language used appropriate to the purpose and the audience?

 Is the layout of the advertisement effective?

 Are all words spelled correctly?

Unit 12 Letter to the Editor

What is a letter to the editor?

Most newspapers and magazines include an editorial page where readers can express their opinions about current issues through letters to the editor. Letters to the editor may seek to criticize, correct, persuade, express appreciation, or question. Some letters identify a new issue; others respond to an article or letter to the editor previously printed in the newspaper or magazine.

Learning Goals

- write a letter to the editor
- make pronouns agree with their antecedents in gender and number
- use correct punctuation, capitalization, and format in letters
- use effective openings
- use strong arguments
- use effective proofreading strategies

The Joy of Just Doing Nothing

BY EMMA MUNRO

YOUR OCT. 8 ARTICLE, TAKING A BREAK FROM THE FAMILY Circus (Life Section), hit the nail on the head. As a high school student preparing to leave home next year, the article made me reflect on some of my fondest memories of growing up.

It was while doing nothing that my family and I would often end up having the most fun. My sister Claire and I had our fair share of piano lessons, softball teams, and visits to "culturally important" places such as theatres or museums. My parents naturally felt the need to try to encourage us in many areas while waiting for our hidden talents and interests to pop up out of nowhere.

But these heartfelt efforts by my parents, though appreciated, aren't the happiest memories I have of growing up. I didn't need my parents to pay for skating lessons to know that they loved me, because I already had Sunday afternoons.

On Sundays we would almost always just hang around. I think my parents sometimes felt bad that we weren't all out "doing something special," but no one really minded. I remember just chatting with my mom in the kitchen as she prepared Sunday dinner and helping her cut up some vegetables. My dad and I would sometimes catch a baseball game on TV and yell in unison if our favourite player made an error.

Sometimes the whole family would go for a walk in the nearby park, but it never seemed forced, or like an obligation. We were actually enjoying ourselves as we talked and collected leaves and threw rocks in the river. Maybe we weren't doing those things and we just ended up doing nothing instead.

Looking back, I know that spending time together on those occasions was really important. You don't always have to be out doing something special. Sometimes the special times are already taking place, and you don't even realize it. ■

Don't Exploit Children

BY CRAIG KIELBURGER

RE "BUYING AN ORIENTAL CARPET," BY JUSTIN BILL (Aug. 13). In Bill's eagerness to help consumers purchase the best Indian or Persian carpet, he drew up several lists of questions and suggestions as a guideline.

Unfortunately, he forgot the most important question of all: Was the carpet made from child labour and the exploitation of children?

Last November, at an international labour conference in Stockholm, Sweden, a young boy from Pakistan, Iqbal Masih, stunted in growth from lack of nourishment and fresh air, told the world how he was sold into slavery at the age of four and shackled to a carpet loom 12 hours a day, six days a week, tying tiny knots, hour after hour, making carpets for consumers in countries like ours.

After six years he was able to escape. This past April, however, at 12 years of age, he was murdered.

Thousands of children work in slave-like conditions in the carpet industry, because their small fingers are best able to make the tiniest knots so much in demand by consumers in the Western world. As your story notes, a 1.5-metre by 2.4-metre carpet with 500 000 knots can cost $5000.

These children often work as bonded labourers. They are taken from their families as collateral for small loans, for as little as $10, by unscrupulous factory owners who charge such high interest rates that the children are enslaved for years.

Following consumer pressure, Germany recently adopted a tag called "Rugmark," which tells consumers that the carpet they are buying was not made from the exploitation of children. Unfortunately, Canada has no such social clause in its trade agreements.

Consumers in Canada must be ready to challenge our government and importers on this important question. Wouldn't we all enjoy our carpets a lot more if we knew they were not made from the exploitation and suffering of children?

Note: A year after this letter was published, Craig Kielburger's Free the Children campaign succeeded in getting "Rugmark" introduced in Canada. ■

Investigating the Models

1. A letter to the editor can be used to criticize, correct, persuade, express appreciation, or question. What purpose does each of the models serve?

2. A letter to the editor usually begins by identifying an issue and expressing an opinion. Identify the opinion or point of view at the beginning of each model. Write one sentence expressing the thesis of each.

3. A good letter to the editor provides detailed arguments to support the general opinion being expressed. For each model, list in point form the arguments that support the writer's opinion, and comment on the effectiveness of these arguments. Which of the two writers do you think makes her or his point most convincingly? Why?

4. Arguments (details) are arranged in an effective order in a letter to the editor. Often, the strongest argument is given close to the end of the letter, so the reader is left with a strong impression. Identify what you think is the strongest argument used in each of the model letters. Has the writer, in your opinion, placed this argument in the best possible position?

5. A letter to the editor often ends with a call to action, a question, or a summary of the main argument. Identify how each of the models ends. Rewrite one of the endings in a different way, and compare your version with that of the writer. Which do you prefer? Why?

6. Although the tone may vary, most letters to the editor are written in formal language. Find proof of this (words, phrasing, etc.) in both of the model letters.

Checkpoint: Letter to the Editor

 As a class, create a checklist of common features of a letter to the editor, based on what you have just learned. Use the checklist to help you write your own letters.

Writer's Workshop

WRITER'S WORKSHOP

Learning Goal

- **write a letter to the editor**

1. Working in groups of four, brainstorm a list of issues relating to your school, community, province, or country. The following prompts may help to get you thinking.

   - I believe there is a better solution to_____.
   - If we could_____, our school (community/ province/ country) would be a better place.
   - There is no reason why_____.

After you have made your list, select the issue you would most like to write about.

IDEA FILE

- Write about an issue that presently concerns you.
- Look for controversial articles in newspapers or magazines.
- Read editorials and letters to the editor.
- Choose a character from literature or history and develop a letter that this person might have written.

2. Decide what group or individual you need to convince in order to realize your purpose. Direct your arguments to that audience.

3. On a separate piece of paper, write one sentence stating your opinion on the issue you have chosen, then list at least three ideas or arguments that you think would be most convincing to your audience. Finally, list facts, examples, or illustrations to back up each argument.

4. Decide on an appropriate order for your arguments. It's a good idea to save your best argument for last, but remember to begin with a strong point in order to draw the reader's attention.

5. Write a draft. As you write, think about your audience: Will they be convinced by these arguments? Is the tone and level of language appropriate?

6. Refer to the list you created at Checkpoint, and revise and edit your letter until you are satisfied with its focus, content, and organization.

Oral Language Extension

Use your letter to the editor as the basis for a short persuasive speech, which you will deliver to a group of three or four of your classmates. You may need to provide more background on the issue, especially if your letter was a response to a letter or article in a newspaper. Also, consider expanding your argument by including more specific examples and illustrations. Make any changes in wording, tone, or language that you feel are necessary in light of your new audience, and practise presenting your speech, using the guidelines in the Speaking Skills section, on page 204.

After each speech, leave time for a general debate of the issue among members of the group. Have someone in the group act as chair, making sure the discussion is focused, avoiding conflicts, and keeping track of the time.

Before passing on to the next speech, each group member should give the speaker feedback, noting one strength of the speech, and suggesting one aspect of the presentation that could be improved.

IDEA FILE

Here are some tips to help you manage a debate or discussion within your group.

- **Separate opinions from facts.** Rather than fight over facts, refer to another source (e.g., an expert, your teacher, reference books) for clarification.
- **Be open to new ideas.** Don't be afraid to change your opinion or admit you were wrong if someone presents a convincing argument.
- **Don't take it personally.** The outcome of conflict does not have to involve one side losing. You can simply "agree to differ."
- **Ask questions and paraphrase.** Sometimes disagreements are based on misunderstandings. Before you confront someone or disagree, make sure you understand what they are saying, by asking them, or by repeating what they said in your own words.
- **Speak for yourself.** Instead of saying, "You are wrong," or "Nobody believes that," say, "I disagree," or "I don't believe that."
- **Wait your turn.** Do not interrupt when someone else is talking. If necessary, have the chair decide whose turn it is to speak.

Grammar

Letters to the editor are usually written in formal language. This means that you need to pay extra attention to correct grammar and word use. Some of the most common grammatical mistakes we make when we speak or write informally involve pronouns. Here is a quick review of pronoun case and agreement.

> A **pronoun** agrees with its antecedent in number and gender.

Be particularly careful when the pronoun replaces an indefinite pronoun such as *everyone, each, both, all, some.*

Wrong:	Each of my sisters has **their** own fondest memory of the family.
Right:	Each of my sisters has **her** own fondest memory of the family.

Pronouns also differ in form, or case, depending on how they are used in a sentence. The three cases of English pronouns are **subjective** (*I, you, he/she/it, we, they, who*), **objective** (*me, you, him/her/it, us, them, whom*), and **possessive** (*mine, yours, his/hers/its, ours, theirs, whose*). While the possessive case rarely gives trouble (just remember not to use an apostrophe before the "s"!), the subjective and objective cases are sometimes confused.

> Use **subjective** pronouns for subjects and subject complements; use **objective** pronouns for direct and indirect objects and as objects of prepositions.

You are most likely to make mistakes in case when the pronoun is part of a compound (joined to another word by *and, or,* or *nor*).

Wrong:	My parents treated *my sister and I* to many cultural experiences.
Right:	My parents treated *my sister and me* to many cultural experiences.
Wrong:	*My friends and me* want to join the Free the Children campaign.

Right: *My friends and I* want to join the Free the Children campaign.

Another common error in case comes in sentences with a linking verb. Although when you speak you probably often say "It's me," rather than "It's I," in formal writing that usage is not acceptable. Use a subjective pronoun for a subject complement.

Wrong: It is *us* who should be willing to challenge the government.

Right: It is *they* who should ask themselves if they are being fair.

> The **antecedent** of the pronoun should be clear to the reader.

Vague antecedents are particularly common when you use *this* or *that* as a pronoun.

Vague: Thousands of children work in slave-like conditions in the carpet industry. *This* is unacceptable.

Better: Thousands of children work in slave-like conditions in the carpet industry. *This situation* is unacceptable.

> Do not use the masculine singular pronoun to refer to people in general.

While the masculine singular pronoun (*he, him*) used to be considered acceptable when referring to people in general, this usage is now outdated. Whenever possible, avoid gender bias by choosing your language—and pronouns—carefully.

Wrong: Every parent should set aside time to do nothing with his children.

Right: Every parent should set aside time to do nothing with his or her children.

OR

All parents should set aside time to do nothing with their children.

In spoken English, you would probably use the plural pronoun *their* in place of *his* or *her* in the above sentence. This solution is acceptable in speech, but not in formal writing. Use *his* or *her*, or change the whole sentence to avoid the problem.

WRITING TIP

In addition to misuse of *he* or *man,* bias can show up in your writing in other more subtle ways. For example, be wary of making broad generalizations or assumptions about particular genders or groups; there will almost always be an exception to your rule.

1. Rewrite the letter below to avoid problems with pronouns.

It seems, according to a recent article (Plaza Bans Teens, September 15) that the owner of Kitgate Plaza, Mr. Solanyi, wants to ban teenagers from the premises because they "create a nuisance." This is simply untrue. My friends and me like to meet at the plaza after school, but we don't "create a nuisance," as the plaza owner claimed. Ask anyone who has visited the plaza while we were there, and they will tell you that we are polite and cause them no trouble.

So why is Mr. Solanyi afraid of us? What have we done to deserve his distrust? He may not like our style of clothing or our hair; everyone is entitled to his own opinion. But that does not mean it is all right to discriminate against my friends and I. It is him who is acting badly, not us.

2. Read over your letter to the editor, and check that the pronouns used in each sentence are in the correct number and case. Also check to see that you have avoided gender bias.

MEDIA LINK

Newspapers often carry cartoons on the editorial page, alongside the letters from readers. These editorial cartoons comment on some issue currently in the news. Every year in late December, the best editorial cartoonists are given awards. Locate some of these award-winning cartoons, and work in small groups to identify what they all have in common, and what makes each stand out. Use what you have learned to draw your own cartoon illustrating the point you made in your letter to the editor, or to comment on another issue of interest to readers your own age.

Mechanics

Follow these basic rules for format and punctuation when you submit your letter to a newspaper or magazine.

> ### *Learning Goal*
>
> - **use correct punctuation, capitalization, and format in letters**

- Note any special instructions regarding submissions, such as maximum or minimum lengths, and make sure you have followed them.

- Write a brief cover letter to introduce your submission. You can either include your editorial in the letter, or attach it on a separate sheet of paper. Follow the style of the sample letter below:

Dear Ms. Mauti:

I am writing to express my opinion on Laura Arciszewski's article, Youth Have Too Much Time on Their Hands (May 5, 2000, p. B4). My letter is attached. I can be reached at 555-4567 after 4:00 p.m. or by e-mail at kirrikh@replay.com.

Sincerely,

- Print the final copy of your letter on a clean, white, standard size sheet of paper.

- Use a typeface that is clear and readable (e.g., Times Roman).

- Always double-space your letter.

- Choose one of the standard letter formats on the following page: block, modified block, or semiblock.

- Use a colon after the salutation and a comma after the closing.

Block

```
_____
_____
_____
Dear _____ :
_____
_____
_____
_____
_____
_____

Yours truly,

_____
```

Modified Block

```
                    _____
                    _____
                    _____
Dear _____ :
_____
_____
_____
_____
_____
_____
                    Yours truly,

                    _____
```

Semiblock

```
_____
_____
_____
Dear _____ :
    _____
_____
    _____

    _____
_____
    _____
Yours truly,

_____
```

- Proofread your letter carefully, double-checking proper names and quotations. Remember that mistakes look much worse in print!

- If you are sending your letter by surface mail rather than e-mail, use the following format to address your envelope.

```
MR. KIAN MERRIKH
987 DEER CROSSING
VICTORIA BC  Z6T 8L3

                    THE VICTORIA BANNER
                    214 HAMPTON STREET
                    VICTORIA BC  Z6T 4T5

                    ATTENTION: LETTERS EDITOR
```

WRITING TIP

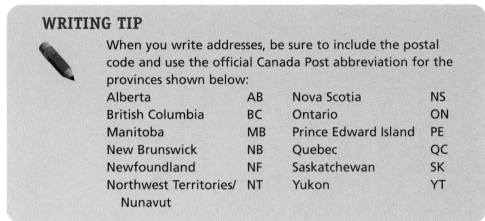

When you write addresses, be sure to include the postal code and use the official Canada Post abbreviation for the provinces shown below:

Alberta	AB	Nova Scotia	NS
British Columbia	BC	Ontario	ON
Manitoba	MB	Prince Edward Island	PE
New Brunswick	NB	Quebec	QC
Newfoundland	NF	Saskatchewan	SK
Northwest Territories/ Nunavut	NT	Yukon	YT

1. Check the format, punctuation, and capitalization of your letter to the editor and envelope using the information outlined in this section, and the class guidelines you developed.

Usage & Style

Here are three ways to make your argument more forcefully in a persuasive letter or essay.

Make every word count.

Avoid weak openings such as these:

> **Learning Goal**
> • use effective openings

Weak: The purpose of this letter is to discuss the recent article about year-round schooling.

Stronger: The recent article about year-round schooling provided very sound reasons for its implementation.

Weak: In this letter I will prove to you that year-round schooling is a good idea.

Stronger: Year-round schooling is a good idea because ...

Weak: This letter will convince you that year-round schooling would benefit our community.

Stronger: Year-round schooling would benefit our community because ...

1. Examine the openings for each of the models. Discuss the effectiveness of each opening.

> Use one or two rhetorical questions to engage your audience.

A rhetorical question is a question for which you do not really expect an answer. They are there to make the reader think, or to spur the audience to action.

> Wouldn't we all enjoy our carpets a lot more if we knew they were not made from the exploitation and suffering of children?

2. Write a suitable rhetorical question that could be used as a heading for one of the model letters. Compare your questions with those of a partner, and discuss the effectiveness of each.

3. Write two rhetorical questions that you used or could use in your own letter to the editor.

> Avoid personal attacks and absolute statements.

Attacking someone's character for the sake of winning points is rarely an effective strategy. Avoid using statements like these:

> Our local MP must be brain dead if he thinks anyone wants this bill to pass.

> People who support this government are either selfish or stupid.

Absolute statements are statements that use words like *never, always, all,* and *impossible.* It is very difficult to justify such statements: an exception can probably be found for most broad generalizations.

Absolute: Parents should always stay home with their children on Sunday afternoons.

Qualified: Parents should sometimes stay home with their children ...

Absolute: Year-round schooling never works.

Qualified: Year-round schooling has not worked in the past.

State your opinions boldly, and back them up with strong arguments.

Learning Goal

• use strong
  arguments

Qualifying your opinions with statements like "In my opinion" or "It seems to me" is redundant, and can reduce the impact of your argument. If you are confident of your opinions and your arguments, don't be afraid to state them.

4. Find three examples of opinions expressed as statements of fact in the model letters, then show how the author(s) have backed up these opinions.

5. Rewrite the following letter, removing unnecessary words, and avoiding absolute statements. Include one effective rhetorical question in your revised version.

   In this letter, I will discuss the issue of year-round schooling. In my opinion, year-round schooling is a good idea, because I think that it would make better use of the space in the classrooms. In addition, I would like to point out that students always forget everything they have learned over the summer holidays. It is clear that this will never be the case if they are in school all year. It seems to me that these benefits make year-round schooling an option worth considering.

6. Check over your letter to the editor to make sure you have not used unnecessary words, and that your arguments are presented forcefully. Make any changes you think are necessary.

Word Study & Spelling

Before you mail your letter to the editor, take special care to proofread it carefully for spelling and punctuation errors. Here are some tips to help you proofread well:

Learning Goal

• use effective
  proofreading
  strategies

• Go slowly. It is easy to miss mistakes in your own work because you already know what you meant to say. Slow your reading down by reading out loud, or following along with your finger or a ruler.

- Read backward. If you read from the end instead of the beginning you are forced to look at each word individually. You are more likely to catch mistakes this way.

- Get another pair of eyes. After you have proofread your work, pass it on to a classmate or friend to check as well.

- Be especially careful with words that have double letters, words with *ie* or *ei*, words that look wrong (even a little bit), long words, and words with silent letters.

- If you are working on the computer, print out a copy of your writing and proofread the hard copy. Computer screens are hard on the eyes, and it is easier to miss or skip words when you work on screen.

- Check and double-check the spelling of people's names. This will be the first thing other people will notice when your letter is published!

- Look through once, focusing only on capitals at the beginning of sentences and end punctuation. You will likely notice some other mistakes as you go.

1. Use the techniques above to proofread your letter to the editor. Then pass it on to a classmate to proofread again. Did he or she find any mistakes that you missed?

2. Create a poster for your classroom showing proofreading symbols. For each symbol, give an example of how to use it.

WORD ORIGINS

As Craig Kielburger's letter implied, India and the countries of the Near East (which used to make up the Persian Empire) are renowned for their beautiful carpets. However, carpets are not the only things we have imported from this region. The English language has also borrowed many words from countries such as India and Iran. For example, that familiar fruit, the **orange**, gets its name from the Persian word *narang*. Here are some other imported words. Look up their meanings and origins in a dictionary.

bungalow   calico   cheetah   curry   pyjamas

Looking Back

Before handing in your final edited draft, have a classmate check your letter to the editor, paying particular attention to the following:

 Are pronouns in the correct case and person?

 Has gender bias in pronouns been avoided?

 Is the format of the covering letter correct?

 Is the envelope properly addressed?

 Is the punctuation and use of capitalization correct?

 Has the writer avoided redundant expressions such as "I think that ..." ?

 Are all words, especially proper names, spelled correctly?

Reflect and Build on Your Learning

Reflecting on Persuasive Writing Forms

1. Review the Learning Goals on page 157. Which goals do you think you have achieved most successfully? Which goals do you think will require you to do more work? Why?

2. This section covered three forms of persuasion. What other forms of persuasive writing do you know? (You may wish to review the features of persuasion on page 156.) Choose one of them and describe its features to a partner, explaining *why* and *when* you would use it. Does your partner agree with your explanation? Would you change anything you've said because of his or her feedback? In what way?

Looking Over Persuasive Writing Forms

1. Working with a small group, discuss what you know about comparisons, advertisements, and letters to the editor. To guide your discussion, create a chart that includes these three forms, as well as the additional form for activity #2 above. Develop five criteria for comparing the forms. One criterion might be the audience for each form. Complete the chart to compare the four forms. Compare your chart with those of other groups. How would you modify your chart based on what they have included in theirs?

CRITERIA	COMPARISON	ADVERTISEMENT	LETTER TO THE EDITOR	OTHER
Audience				

Using the Persuasive Writing Forms

1. Write a short essay comparing the presentation of a historical event in a textbook and in a work of fiction. As you write and revise, use as a guide the class checklist of features for comparisons. Edit and proofread your essay, especially for the checklist of items on page 171.

2. Working with a small group, find an example of an advertisement or a book cover (front and back) that is intended to appeal to an identifiable audience. Using as a guide the class checklist of features for advertisements, evaluate the effectiveness for the intended audience of the advertisement or cover. Now decide on a different audience for your advertisement or cover. Make a two-column chart listing on one side the profile characteristics (age group, gender, etc.) of the new audience, and on the other side the information you want to convey across to that audience. Redesign the advertisement or cover to suit the new audience, again using the class checklist as a guide. Any images you include may be in rough form, but any words you use must be carefully edited and proofread, especially for the checklist of items on page 185. Present your advertisement or cover to the class, explaining your redesign.

3. Working with a partner, identify an issue that is of strong current interest in your community. Scan recent issues of newspapers for letters to the editor on the issue, collecting about six of these letters. Paste these letters on to chart paper for a class presentation on the features and coverage of these letters. In your presentation, identify the issue clearly and show how the letters express different points of views on it.

4. Write a research report on explicit and implicit messages in television sitcoms or in advertisements aimed at the youth market. Use as guides both the class checklist for advertisements and the class checklist for research reports. Locate and summarize information from resources such as media and marketing magazines, television shows, and the Internet, organizing the information into interesting subtopics. When you write your report, provide an introduction, body, conclusion, and a brief bibliography. Ask a classmate to check a complete draft of your report to ensure that it is interesting to readers, well organized, and provides enough facts and examples for each subtopic. Revise your report as needed, and have your classmate edit and proofread it carefully, especially for the checklist of items on page 153.

Speaking Skills

Even the most famous actors have suffered from stage fright at one time or another. This may be little consolation to you if you are worried about making your own oral presentation, but you can practise some simple techniques that will help you speak more effectively before an audience.

- Focus on the purpose of your presentation. Understand what it is you have to say and why you are saying it.

- Write key words or phrases on a single cue card. Avoid putting your entire presentation on cue cards as this increases the tendency to read it.

- Rehearse your presentation over and over again—in front of a mirror, on videotape, and/or in front of family members or friends.

- Take time to relax before you get up to speak. Try stretching to relax tight muscles, which in turn will relax you. Or find a quiet place where you can sit, close your eyes, take slow, regular breaths, and visualize yourself in a setting where you are comfortable and relaxed. Try to keep this feeling with you when you get up to speak.

- Pause for a moment before you start, to settle the audience (and yourself). If possible, pause after important statements to heighten their effect and help you maintain regular breathing.

- Speak from your diaphragm, just below your rib cage, rather than from your throat.

- Breathe slowly, speak slowly. Nervousness results in shallow, rapid breathing that can make you speak too fast. Force yourself to take slow, regular breaths.

- Maintain a comfortable posture. Stand straight with your feet slightly apart, and give your hands something to do so they don't fidget (e.g., hold a glass of water, or keep one hand in your pocket).

- Make eye contact. Select three people seated in different parts of the room and allow your gaze to wander from one to the next. This will give the impression that you are looking at everyone.

Listening Skills

Hearing and listening are very different acts. Hearing is a passive activity in which our ears merely receive sound waves. Listening, on the other hand, involves actively thinking about the sounds we hear. Here are some techniques you can practise to help you become a more effective listener.

Before you listen ...

- Identify your purpose for listening. What will you be expected to do with the information you hear? (Write a report? Present the information to someone else? Write a test?)
- Make a point-form list of what you already know about the topic to be discussed.
- Anticipate what the speaker will say about this topic.

While you are listening ...

- Watch the face of the person speaking or acting.
- Listen for clues that show how the speaker has organized the information. For example, he or she may identify three main points, or introduce a problem that requires a solution, or describe a cause that has a particular effect.
- Try to create mental pictures of the things that are being said.
- Ask yourself questions about what you are hearing.
- Take notes. You might try sketching a framework (for example, problem-solution, cause-effect) and briefly filling in details as the speaker provides them; listing key words and then adding details provided about these key words; or drawing circles and arrows, to cluster related ideas.

After you have listened ...

- Make sure your notes are clear and legible. If not, rewrite them in a more organized manner, adding any other important details that you remember.
- Jot down any questions you may have about things you are not sure of, and make a note to clarify these later.

Transitional Expressions

Transitions are words or phrases that help guide a reader through a piece of writing by showing how two or more ideas are related. Here is a list of common transitions, grouped according to the functions they perform:

Transitions that show order: first, second, third, fourth, next, finally

Transitions that show a time sequence: after a while, afterward, at last, at length, during, eventually, immediately, in the future, in the past, later, meanwhile, soon, today, tomorrow, next week, yesterday, until, when

Transitions that show importance: the least important, the most significant, a major factor, a minor consideration

Transitions that show a cause and effect: accordingly, as a result, because, consequently, for this reason, since, therefore, thus

Transitions that show a comparison: again, also, by way of comparison, in a similar way, likewise, similarly

Transitions that show a contrast: although, at the same time, but, despite this, even though, however, in contrast, in spite of, instead, nevertheless, one difference, on the contrary, on the other hand, still, though

Transitions that show location: above, across, along, around, behind, below, beneath, beyond, elsewhere, near, farther, here, there, inside, outside, in front of, in back of, on top of, on the other side, opposite

Transitions that emphasize or reinforce: additionally, again, also, at the same time, besides, equally important, furthermore, in addition, in fact, lastly, moreover

Transitions that clarify: for example, for instance, in other words, in particular, for this reason, specifically

Transitions that summarize: in brief, in conclusion, in general, in short, in summary, with this in mind

Key Words in Assignments and Tests

Listed below are some key words that you may come across in assignments, homework questions, and tests, along with a brief explanation of what they mean.

Analyze: Divide into parts and explain the relationship of the parts to each other, and of the parts to the whole.

Argue: Make a statement or express an opinion and support it with evidence.

Classify: Separate ideas or items into groups with similar characteristics.

Compare: Use examples to show how two things are similar and different.

Contrast: Use examples to show how two things are different.

Criticize: State your opinion of the correctness or goodness of an item or issue.

Debate: Consider, discuss, or argue the affirmative or negative sides of a statement or proposition.

Define: Give the meaning of the word or subject, the group or class to which it belongs, its function, and how it is different from the others in that group.

Describe: Tell how something or someone looks, feels, sounds, etc. Give vivid details to create a word picture.

Discuss: Examine and analyze a topic from all sides and try to form a conclusion or thesis. Give reasons pro and con.

Evaluate: Give your opinion of the value or worth of an idea or subject. Include both the good points and the bad points.

Explain: Tell how or why something happens or show how something works.

List: Provide examples, reasons, causes, or other details in list form.

Prove: Present facts and details that show clearly that something is true.

Relate: Show how two or more things are connected.

Review: Give an overall picture or summary of the most important points.

State: Use brief sentences to present your ideas about a subject.

Summarize: Present the main points in a clear, concise form.

Commonly Misused Words

The following chart contains some commonly misused words. If other words are causing you difficulty, consult a usage handbook or dictionary.

WORDS	USAGE	EXAMPLES
accept	receive (verb)	I accept your offer to help.
except	exclude (preposition)	Everyone except me came on time.
affect	influence (verb)	Her injury affected her performance.
effect	result (noun)	The storm had no effect on the crops.
	cause (verb)	The storm effected a change in our plans.

already	previously	Our ride to the game has already gone.
all ready	completely ready	I think we're all ready to go.
among	applies to two or more objects	He walked among the people.
between	applies to only two objects	Why don't you sit between us?
amount	refers to quantity	That is a large amount of money.
number	refers to things	A large number of students attended.
borrow	take	May I borrow your pen?
lend	give	Meagan will lend me her notes.
bring	carry toward the speaker	Bring that book to me.
take	carry away from the speaker	Take this message to the office.
complement	complete or make perfect	Those colours really complement each other.
compliment	praise a person	My teacher complimented me on my performance.
emigrate	leave a country	He emigrated from Portugal.
immigrate	enter a country	She immigrated to Canada.
farther	greater in space or distance	They travelled two kilometres farther.
further	greater in degree or time	We need to talk further on that topic.

fewer	a smaller number (amounts that can be counted)	We have fewer holidays now.
less	a smaller quantity (amounts that can't be counted)	There is less milk in my glass than in yours.
good	(adjective)	I feel good.
well	(adverb)	You don't look well.
in	within a place	I'll meet you in the cafeteria.
into	motion from one place to another	She fell into the pool.
later	after some time	I got home later than usual.
latter	second of the two	The latter of the answers is correct.
loose	not tight (adjective)	This jacket feels loose on me.
lose	misplace (verb)	How did you lose your money?
maybe	perhaps (adverb)	Maybe it will rain tomorrow.
may be	could be (verb phrase)	We may be able to go tomorrow.
passed	go by (verb)	We passed them on the highway.
past	the time before the present (noun)	Don't worry about the past.
quiet	silent (adjective)	Try to keep quiet while I am studying.
quite	very (adverb)	Our school performed quite well.

Common Homophones

Homophones are words that sound alike but have different spellings and meanings. Homophones usually come in pairs, but they also come in groups of three or more. Below is a list of some homophones that you should understand and be able to spell. Check meanings you are unsure of in a dictionary, and add them to a personal list of words to learn.

air/heir
ant/aunt
ate/eight
bare/bear
base/bass
be/bee
berry/bury
blew/blue
bough/bow
brake/break
by/buy/bye
ceiling/sealing
cell/sell
cent/scent/sent/
cereal/serial
cite/sight/site
coarse/course
council/counsel
creak/creek
currant/current
earn/urn
fair/fare
fir/fur

flea/flee
flour/flower
for/fore/four
foul/fowl
gnu/knew/new
grate/great
groan/grown
hair/hare
heal/heel/he'll
hear/here
heard/herd
hole/whole
hour/our
its/it's
know/no
lead/led
mail/male
one/won
pail/pale
pain/pane
pair/pare/pear
peace/piece
plain/plane

principal/principle
rain/reign/rein
read/red
right/rite/write
sail/sale
scene/seen
sew/so/sow
stair/stare
stake/steak
heir/there/they're
threw/through
to/too/two
toe/tow
wail/whale
waist/waste
ware/wear/where
way/weigh
weak/week
weather/whether
who's/whose
wood/would
your/you're

MLA Style for Bibliographies

Here are some examples of citations for a bibliography. Most are written in MLA (Modern Language Association) style, although some citations have been simplified slightly.

A book by a single author
Include the author's name, the title of the book, the place of publication, the publisher, and the date it was published. You will find this information on the copyright page.

Wong, Sylvia. <u>Flying Squirrels: Fact and Fiction</u>. Toronto: Nuthatch, 1999.

A book by two or more authors
Runan, Jackie, and Walter Hide. <u>Tales of Embarrassment</u>. Calgary: Redface, 1998.

A work in an anthology
Include the page numbers at the end of the citation as shown.

Spring, Debbie. "The Kayak." <u>Takes: Stories for Young Adults</u>.
    Ed. R. P. McIntyre. Saskatoon: Thistledown Press, 1996. 106–111.

A reference book
If the article is signed by an author, start the entry with his or her name. Otherwise, begin with the title of the article itself.

Gadakz, Rene R. "Kayak." <u>The Canadian Encyclopedia</u>. 2nd ed. 1988.

"Martial Arts." <u>Merriam-Webster's Collegiate Dictionary</u>. 10th ed. 1993.

A pamphlet
<u>Sightseeing Destinations</u>. Halifax: Department of Tourism, 2000.

A newspaper or magazine article

If the article is continued on pages later in the magazine, write a plus sign after the first page number, as shown.

Valerie Hill. "Guelph Teen Makes Mark on In-Line Skating Circuit."
Kitchener-Waterloo Record 7 Oct. 1998: C6.

Eric Harris, "Struck Powerless." Canadian Geographic Mar.–Apr. 1998: 30+.

A CD-ROM

The CIA World Factbook. CD-ROM. Minneapolis: Quanta, 1992.

Godard, Barbara. "Margaret Eleanor Atwood." The 1999 Canadian
Encyclopedia. World ed. CD-ROM. Toronto: McClelland & Stewart, 1999.

A web site

Include the date you accessed the information, and enclose the web address in angle brackets: < >.

"Going Bananas." National Post Online. 9 Apr. 1999
<www.nationalpost.com>

Wang, Kim. Home page. 1 Dec. 2000. <www.webcity/personal/wang.htm>

Television or radio show

Include the title of the episode or segment, the title of the program and of the series, if applicable, the name of the network, and the date the show was broadcast.

"Dead Heat." The Nature of Things. Host David Suzuki. CBC Television.
4 Mar. 1999.

"The Men Who Invented the Universe." Ideas. Host Lister Sinclair.
Narr. Max Allen. CBC Radio One. 20 Jan. 1999.

A film or video

Bob's Birthday. Created by Richard Fine and Alison Snowdon.
Videocassette. National Film Board of Canada, 1993.

Frequently Misspelled Words

about	because*	chases	especially
accident	been	children	ever
actually	before	climbed	every
afraid	began	come	everybody
again*	behind	coming	everyday
all	believe	could	everything
almost	better	couldn't	exciting
always	bird	cousins	family
and	birthday	decided	fell
animals	brought	didn't*	few
another*	built	different	field
are	buys	doctor	finally
around	bye	does	finished
away	came	doesn't	fired
awhile	can't	dollars	first
back	catch	don't	flowers
bear	caught*	engine	for
beautiful*	certainly	equipment	found

* 25 words most frequently misspelled

friend*	knew	one	said*
funny	know*	opportunity	saw
girls	let's*	others	scared
going	like	our*	school
government	lived	out	screamed
happened	looked	outside	second
happily	met	parents	shoot
having	middle	parliament	shot
heard*	might	people	situation
here	minute	picked	slept
him	months	pictures	so
his	mountains	piece	society
hole	myself	place	some
home	names	pollution	something*
horses	necessary	practising	sometimes
hospital	neighbour	pretty	spotted
house	next	probably	started
I'm	no	quiet	stepped
Indians	nothing	quite	stopped
into*	now	really	strange
it's*	o'clock	receive	summer
its	off*	responsible	surely
just	once	right	surprise

swimming	there's	tried	we're
take	they*	turned	were*
than	they're	two	weren't
that's*	things	until	what's
the	thought	upon*	when*
their*	threw	very	where*
them	throw	wanted	without
then	to	wasn't	wouldn't
there*	too	went*	writing

Index

Acknowledgments

Photographs

Page 18 PhotoDisc; page 19 PhotoDisc; page 20 PhotoDisc; page 32 PhotoDisc; page 33 PhotoDisc; page 34 PhotoDisc; page 35 PhotoDisc; page 37 PhotoDisc; page 48 PhotoDisc; page 49 PhotoDisc; page 51 Comstock; page 66 PhotoDisc; page 67 PhotoDisc; page 68 PhotoDisc; page 69 Comstock; page 82 Comstock; page 83 The Record; page 84 PhotoDisc; page 96 Dick Hemingway; page 97 PhotoDisc; page 98 Canapress; page 114 Comstock; page 126 Comstock; page 127 Comstock; page 128 Comstock; page 129 PhotoDisc; page 140 Comstock; page 141 PhotoDisc; page 142 Comstock; page 160 (both) PhotoDisc; page 161 Comstock; page 162 Comstock; page 174 Corel; page 176 PhotoDisc; page 188 Dick Hemingway; page 189 PhotoDisc; page 190 Canapress

Text

"A Flying Start" by Margaret Atwood. Reprinted with the permission of Stoddart Publishing, Toronto, Ontario. "The Kayak" by Debbie Spring from *Takes: Stories for Young Adults* (Thistledown Press, 1996). Word Study & Spelling, from *Patterns of Communication.* Reprinted by permission of Allan Glatthorn. "Odd Jobs" by Frank Moher. "Odd Jobs" is published by Blizzard Publishing/International reading Theatre. "Neither Out Far Nor In Deep" from THE POETRY OF ROBERT FROST, edited by Edward Connery Lathem, Copyright 1936 by Robert Frost, Copyright Lesley Frost Ballantine. Copyright 1969 by Henry Holt and Company, Inc. Reprinted by permission of Henry Holt and Company, Inc. "Energy" by Leona Gom from The Collected Poems by Leona Gom, 1991. Reprinted by permission of Sono Nis Press. "Fingerprints" by Kim A. Johnson. Reprinted by permission of the author. "Guelph Teen Makes Mark on In-Line Skating Circuit" by Valerie Hill. Reprinted by permission of the author. "Struck Powerless" by Eric Harris/Canadian Geographic. "Why Rainbows Must Be Curved" by Ira Flatow from RAINBOWS, CURVEBALLS And Other Wonders of the Natural World Explained, by Ira Flatow. Text: Copyright 1988 by Ira Flatow. By permission of William Morrow, Company Inc. "When Machines Think" by Ray Kurzweil from "The Age of Spiritual Machines, When Computers Exceed Human Intelligence". Published by Viking. Reprinted by permission of the author. "The Way of the Empty Hand" by Jill Peacock. Copyright: Young People's Press. Reprinted with permission – The Toronto Star Syndicate. "Neat People vs. Sloppy People" by Suzanne Britt. Reprinted by permission of the author. Milk Web site: Permission courtesy of BSMG Worldwide. Milk ad: Courtesy of Dairy Farmers of Ontario. Photo: Michel Pilon. Agency: BBDO. Art Director: Jim Burt. Writer: Graham Watt. "The Joy of Just Doing Nothing" by Emma Munro. Courtesy of Emma Munro, OAC student (Leaside High School). "Don't Exploit Children" by Craig Kielburger appeared in August 26, 1995 issue of The Toronto Star. Reprinted with permission of the author.